The Story of the Dictionary

by the same author

Crystals of Life: The Story of Salt
(published by Doubleday & Company)

Silent Sentinels: The Story of Locks, Vaults and Burglar Alarms
(published by Doubleday & Company)

The Treason of Benedict Arnold, September 1780
(published by Franklin Watts)

The Statue of Liberty Comes to America
(published by Garrard Publishing Company)

America the Beautiful: Stories of Patriotic Songs
(published by Garrard Publishing Company)

Harry Houdini: Master of Magic
(published by Garrard Publishing Company)

The
Story
of
the
Dictionary

by
Robert Kraske

ILLUSTRATED WITH PHOTOGRAPHS

New York and London

Harcourt Brace Jovanovich

Library of Congress Cataloging in Publication Data

Kraske, Robert.
The story of the dictionary.

Bibliography: p.
Includes index.
SUMMARY: Traces the history of the dictionary and describes what goes
into the compilation of this second most popular book in the English
language.
1. English language—Lexicography—Juvenile literature. [1. English language—Lexicography] I. Title.
PE1611.K7   413'.028   74-23177
ISBN 0-15-280850-7

For Joe Kneeland

Acknowledgments

Many people supplied information for this book, but I would especially like to acknowledge the generous assistance of Duncan G. Steck, Anna M. Rosenberg Associates, New York; Crawford Lincoln, Vice President and Secretary, G. & C. Merriam Company, Springfield, Massachusetts; Earle R. Steinmetz, Advertising Writer for Dictionaries, Scott, Foresman and Company, Glenview, Illinois; and Alma Graham, Executive Editor, Dictionary Division, American Heritage Publishing Company, Inc., New York.

Photographs of dictionary editorial operations are courtesy of G. & C. Merriam Company, publishers of the Merriam-Webster dictionaries; and also courtesy of the Houghton Mifflin Company, publishers of *The American Heritage Dictionary of the English Language* and *The American Heritage School Dictionary*.

I would also like to thank the following publishers for supplying photographic material for use in this book: Scott, Foresman and Company; Random House; Oxford University Press; and Funk & Wagnalls.

Contents

The Story of the Dictionary

Chapter One

The Famous Book
No One Reads

One morning a sixth grader went to his school library and borrowed a dictionary. The same afternoon he returned it.

"Something wrong?" the librarian asked.

"It's a very interesting book," he told her, "but I didn't read it. The stories are too short."

The sixth grader was mistaken about finding stories in the dictionary, but he was right about something else.

Although every school and library and most homes own a dictionary, no one ever reads it—at least not page by page, like a mystery story or a science book.

The fact that no one reads the dictionary doesn't surprise the people who make dictionaries. "A dictionary is hardly a book to read," one dictionary maker said, "but it's a marvelous book to browse in."

Browse means "to nibble at, to glance here and there through a book," which is what we're going to do in *The Story of the Dictionary*—browse through the dictionary, pausing here and there to look at some interesting stories behind this famous book, such as:

* How words get into the dictionary—and why others drop out.

* Who makes dictionaries—and who made the first dictionary for children.

* What the Sears, Roebuck catalog, restaurant menus, and

3

instructions for putting toys together have to do with making dictionaries.

  * How the name of England's most famous hangman entered the language.

  * Why no one knows how many words there are in English and why the longest word does *not* appear in the dictionary. (If you think it's *supercalifragilisticexpialidocious,* you're in for a surprise.)

  * What happened when one dictionary maker insisted that we spell *dumb* without the *b* (dum) and *feather* without the *a* (fether).

  * Why a writer of definitions would ask a question like this: "Does an anteater eat anything but ants?"

  * How a detective from the New York Police Department helped one dictionary maker.

  * What simple three-letter word you use everyday has 213 different meanings.

  * Where the largest word bank in the world is located—and what a word bank is.

  * What caught one dictionary maker's eye in the following sentence: "If you are not satisfied with our product, your money will be cheerfully refunded."

  * Why today's dictionaries are made with the help of giant computers.

  * Why a dictionary maker said: "Dictionaries are like watches: the worst is better than none, and the best cannot be expected to go quite true."

A dictionary is a book about words, and words make up a language. Therefore, as we browse through the dictionary, we will discover some interesting facts about the language we speak and read—how English became the world's most widely spoken language and why, despite its popularity, it is one of the most difficult languages to spell. (This you may already know.)

Finally, you will discover something else—namely, that learning about words and language doesn't necessarily have to be dull stuff. A famous dictionary maker once said, "When you're in this business, it helps if you have a keen sense of humor!"

Most people don't know it, but there are over 250 different kinds of dictionaries. To name a few: a folklore dictionary, a medical dictionary, a rhyming dictionary, a foreign-language dictionary, a tobacco dictionary. There is even a *Dictionary of Sea Slang of the Twentieth Century* and a *Dictionary of Embroidery Stitches*. Each of these special dictionaries presents information on a certain subject.

Here are three more examples:

The *Insult Dictionary* lists all kinds of not-so-nice names—like "hairy creep"—that people call other people in five languages: German, French, Italian, Spanish, and English.

The *Dictionary of the Underworld* records the special vocabulary of crooks, racketeers, beggars, and tramps.

If you enjoy playing word games, get yourself *A Dictionary of Difficult Words*. In it, you will find 15,000 little-known words—like *ghoom, ramellose, frinqilline,* and *quagga*—guaranteed to help you stump the other players.

But the kind of dictionary you will read about in this book is a wordbook, the kind you use at home and in school to look up words. Here is what one dictionary had to say about itself: "A book containing a selection of words of a language . . . usually arranged alphabetically, with explanations of their meanings and other information concerning them; a lexicon, a glossary."

The dictionary is the second most popular book in the English language. Every year, bookstores sell more copies of it than any other book except the Bible. Over 60 million dictionaries can be found in American homes, about one for every four people. At least 87 out of every 100 homes have a dictionary of one kind or another. Still more dictionaries are used every day in schools, libraries, and business offices. No one can even guess the total number in use today.

Dictionaries come in different sizes. Some are small enough

to fit in your pocket and cost less than $1. The largest dictionary takes up a whole bookshelf, weighs over a hundred pounds, and costs more than $300.

The basic difference among dictionaries is the number of words they contain. A dictionary for kindergartners—actually pictures with labels—includes about 500 words; a first grader's dictionary, 800 words. A second grader will use a dictionary with 3,500 entries—words plus definitions. Third and fourth graders will have 18,000-20,000 words in their dictionary; fifth through eighth graders, about 60,000 words.

The next dictionaries up the word scale are for high schools, colleges, homes, and business offices. They carry not fewer than 130,000 words.

Now come the heavyweights. Called unabridged dictionaries, these massive volumes hold between a quarter of a million and half a million entry words in 2,000 to 3,000 pages.

An unabridged dictionary includes every word used by most people for all practical purposes. Left out are scientific or medical terms that only a few people like scientists or doctors might use. Special dictionaries carry these words.

One unabridged dictionary in use today is *Webster's Third New International Dictionary*. It carries 450,000 entries in 2,662 pages and weighs almost 14 pounds. It includes all words used in the English language since the year 1755.

Another popular unabridged dictionary is *The Random House Dictionary of the English Language,* which presents 260,000 entry words in 2,090 pages. Among other features are a 64-page atlas of the world in full color, four foreign-language dictionaries (French, Spanish, Italian, and German), names and dates of historical events, a directory of colleges and universities in the United States and abroad, Biblical names, famous mottoes and proverbs, and the names of Presidents and Vice Presidents of the United States.

The world champion dictionary, though, is *The Oxford English*

Dictionary. Dictionary makers call it "the grandest work of scholarship and research in the English language."

Published in 1928, the OED took 71 years to write, has 16,569 pages in 13 volumes, weighs 105 pounds, and traces every word in the English language back for 10 centuries. Later in this book you will read more about this king of dictionaries.

The dictionaries we use today are products of modern book-making methods. The first dictionaries didn't look at all like the one we use today. In fact, the first dictionaries weren't even in book form.

Chapter Two

The Bright Monks and the Not-So-Bright Monks: The First Dictionary Makers

There is a good deal of myth and misunderstanding about people who make dictionaries. We generally think of them as dry, serious scholars who spend their days in quiet libraries paging through dusty books.

One legend tells of a dictionary maker at work in his study. A knock sounded on the door. He rose from his desk, opened the door, strangled the stranger, and returned to his beloved books.

Myths like this probably started with the early dictionary makers who really did spend their days in quiet libraries absorbed in books. They were monks, men who lived in a religious brotherhood. Sometime in the seventh century—nearly 1,400 years ago and before the printing press was invented—these monks working in church libraries began making notes in the margins of their beautiful hand-lettered books.

In those days, all books were written in Latin. Latin was the language used in the Church and in universities. Common folk— farmers, shopkeepers, tradesmen, children—had no books of their own.

Why did monks mark up the pages of these beautiful books? Because the bright monks who wrote the books wanted to tell the not-so-bright monks who read them what certain words meant. The notes came to be called *glosses*, from which we get our word *glossary*—a list of words with definitions.

For a thousand years, these glosses stayed in the books in church libraries. No one ever did anything with them. Then, in the seventeenth century, some monks got the idea of making lists of these Latin glosses and translating them into English.

So the first dictionary, or glossary, was actually a list of Latin-English glosses. Monks in other countries followed suit and compiled Latin-French, Latin-Italian, and Latin-Spanish glossaries.

Then, in 1604, an English gentleman named Robert Cawdrey published a dictionary. He titled it *A Table Alphabeticall . . . of hard usual English Wordes.* The book was intended, Cawdrey wrote on the title page, "for the benefit and helpe of Ladies, Gentlewomen" and "other unskilfull persons."

His dictionary included only difficult words, but there is one principle of dictionary making that Cawdrey is remembered for today: he listed words in alphabetical order.

Nineteen years later, another Englishman, Henry Cockeram, published his *New Interpreter of Hard English Words.* The purpose of his dictionary, he wrote, was to assist readers to "a speedy attaining of an Elegant Perfection" in their speech. "Elegant Perfection," he said, was for those who "study rather to hear themselves speak than to understand themselves"—which shows that people haven't changed all that much between Cockeram's day and our own.

Cockeram did no research on how people used words. He simply made up his own definitions. For *crocodile*, he wrote: "A beast hatched of an egge, yet some of them grow to a great bignesse, as 10, 20, or 30 foot in length: it hath cruell teeth and a scaly back, with very sharpe clawes on his feete: if it see a man afraid of him, it will pursue him . . ."

Cawdrey and Cockeram wrote their dictionaries for educated people only. Why write a dictionary for uneducated farmers and shopkeepers? They had no use for a dictionary anyway.

Then, in 1721, Nathaniel Bailey wrote his *Universal Etymological English Dictionary*—a history of words rather than a word-book dictionary—and something unusual happened. The English people—the same shopkeepers, farmers, and tradesmen who

Cawdrey and Cockeram said would never use a dictionary—began buying Bailey's dictionary. It became a best-seller and was reprinted thirty times, a remarkable record for any book even today.

Twenty-five years after it was published, Bailey's dictionary was still selling. This fact—and the enormous sums of money the book earned over these years—did not go unnoticed by a group of London publishers. These publishers had a leader, Lord Philip Chesterfield.

"Look here," Chesterfield said to his friends. "If the common folk are so eager for a dictionary, let's give 'em a real dictionary!"

The dictionary he had in mind would list words in alphabetical order—Cawdrey's idea from years before—and provide a definition for each one.

"Splendid idea," his friends said. They could just see the money rolling in. But hold on! Who could write such a dictionary? It wasn't like writing a storybook, they told him. It took someone special.

Lord Chesterfield smiled. "Trust me, fellows," he said. "I know just the man."

Chapter Three

Samuel Johnson: The First Great Dictionary Maker

The man Lord Chesterfield hired to write the new dictionary was Samuel Johnson. Large, fleshy, untidy, his powdered wig askew on his big head, he was a man of immense learning, self-confidence, and sharp—sometimes savage—wit.

Working for a living didn't much interest Johnson. Once he tried running a school near Lichfield, but it soon failed. "Schoolmastering," he told friends, "is a very good profession—to get out of!"

He earned a slim income in London writing poetry, essays, and biographies for *Gentleman's Magazine*, but he spent most of his days in taverns talking with friends. "I look upon every day to be lost," he said, "in which I do not make a new acquaintance."

When Lord Chesterfield offered a down payment of 1,575 pounds to write a dictionary, Johnson accepted gladly. He needed the money—he had a wife to support. Tetty was twenty years his senior, a fat, easy-going companion whom he loved dearly. Unlike Johnson, Tetty was neat and orderly. "A clean floor is *so* comfortable," she said by way of gently scolding her careless husband.

So confident was Johnson of his literary powers that he offered to write the dictionary in three years. Friends warned him that this wasn't time enough. It had taken forty French scholars forty years to write a French dictionary. Shouldn't he reconsider?

"Nonsense," Johnson replied in effect. "Any Englishman is the equal of forty Frenchmen. Three years! That's all it will take."

Despite his casual attitude toward his task, Johnson had firm opinions about dictionary making. A dictionary, he said, should "fix" the pronunciation of words. It should "preserve" the purity of the language, save it from "corruption and decay," and hold back the flood of "low terms" he heard all around him on London streets and in the taverns. The language of common people, he stated, was all too common! His dictionary would include only those words he thought good and keep out those he thought bad.

One afternoon in 1747, having breakfasted at noon, his usual hour for getting out of bed, he huffed up the narrow stairway to the attic of his home at No. 17 Gough Square. Seating himself at a small table and using crude paper and a goose quill pen, he began work.

In writing definitions, Johnson introduced something new. Unlike Cawdrey, Cockeram, or Bailey, he searched books for words to include in his dictionary and also for sentences to show how authors used these words. The written word, he believed, was the keystone of language; all spoken language should sound like sentences in books.

For some words, he wrote his own definitions, sometimes adding a touch of humor.

A dictionary maker, he wrote, was "a harmless drudge."

To illustrate the word *dull,* he wrote: "To make dictionaries is dull work."

One of Johnson's pet peeves—and he had many—was Scotland. "The noblest prospect which a Scotchman ever sees," he said to friends in a tavern one day, "is the high road that leads him to England." In his dictionary, for the word *oats,* he wrote: "Oats is a grain, which in England is generally given to horses, but in Scotland supports the people."

Many of his definitions were hard to understand. For *cough,* he wrote: "A convulsion of the lungs, vellicated by some sharp serosity."

For *network:* "Any thing reticulated or decussated, at equal distances, with interstices between the intersections."

To "preserve" the purity of the language, and simply because he enjoyed their sound, he included words used by writers and poets that most people would never use: *clancular, incompossible, lubrical, magnificate, ventosity.*

In 1755, Johnson finished *A Dictionary of the English Language* —eight years of "sluggishly treading the track of the alphabet," he told friends, not three—and he wasn't at all satisfied with the work he produced. But during those years, he had learned a lot about words and how they make up language.

For one thing, he realized that relying on his memory for definitions wasn't good enough for dictionary making. One day a woman asked him why he had defined *pastern* as the "knee of a horse" (actually the bones just above the hoof). Johnson casually replied, "Ignorance, Madam, pure ignorance." But to friends he confided, "I trusted more to memory than memory can contain."

For another, he no longer thought it possible to "fix" the language. It was like trying to "lash the wind," he said. Language, he discovered, constantly changed. People used the same words to mean different things, and, in time, words took on new meanings. A dictionary recorded the language only for the year in which it was published. Next year the language would be different. Dictionaries, he realized, were out of date as soon as they were printed.

But the most important conclusion Johnson came to was about the nature of language itself. Before beginning his dictionary, he believed that the written word was the foundation of language. Now he realized that it was people and the way in which they used words—spoken English, not books—that determined how language developed. "The pen," he said, "must at length comply with the tongue."

Did Johnson let the defects in his work bother him? Not at all. "Dictionaries are like watches," he said. "The worst is better than none, and the best cannot be expected to go quite true."

Despite his doubts, *A Dictionary of the English Language*—in two volumes 12 inches wide by 19 inches high with 41,000 definitions—was a huge success. Copies soon graced library tables in mansions all over England. A one-volume short version was purchased by shopkeepers, farmers, and tradesmen, the very people whose manner of speaking Johnson had once ignored. Lord Chesterfield was very pleased by the money the dictionary earned.

Johnson's work was a landmark in the history of dictionary making. It was the first time anyone had put down on paper the words that made up the English language, and it set basic guides for the craft of dictionary making. Lexicographers for the next two centuries would follow the principles Johnson—the intellectual, storyteller, and idler in taverns—had established.

Chapter Four

Noah Webster: The Man Who Made America's First Dictionary

One American who objected to the personal style of Samuel Johnson's dictionary was a sober, pious New England schoolmaster named Noah Webster. "Johnson was always depressed by poverty," he said tartly. "He was naturally indolent and seldom wrote until he was urged by want. Hence . . . he was compelled to prepare his manuscripts in haste."

The judgment was hard, but so—when it came to dictionary making—was Noah Webster. In his view, dictionary making allowed no compromise, permitted no weakness. Webster set a standard for excellence in dictionary making that continues to this day.

He was born on a Connecticut farm in 1758. During the Revolutionary War he joined the state militia and in 1777 marched to the fighting at Saratoga. By the time his company arrived, though, the battle was over. Webster and the other men turned around and marched home again.

He attended Yale College and, five years after graduation, in 1783, published his *Blue-Back Speller*, America's first speller, grammar, and reader.

This book sold an amazing million copies a year at a time when the entire population of the United States was only 23 million. It stayed in print over a century (under the titles *The American Spelling Book* and later *The Elementary Spelling Book*) and sold a total of 70 million copies.

The money the book earned freed Webster from the need to work for a living. He could spend his time doing what he really wanted—write dictionaries.

To train for the task, he set about studying languages and in time learned twenty-six, including Anglo-Saxon and Sanskrit.

The basic reason Americans needed a dictionary of their own, Webster believed, was that American English was different from the English of Johnson's day. Settlers in this country had spoken English for two centuries and had invented their own words to describe conditions in this new land.

Imagine an English girl in 1800 visiting a cousin in Virginia. "How are things, John? What did you do this day?"

"Well, I cleared the *underbrush* and a few *hickories* in the *backwoods*, planted *squash*, hunted *bullfrogs*, *muskrats*, and *raccoons*—got scared off by a *skunk* down by the *rapids*, though—and all this after lunching on *johnnycake* and *applesauce*."

The two relatives would be speaking the same language, but the English girl wouldn't have the slightest idea what her American cousin was talking about. And this was why Webster believed American English needed a dictionary. American English, he said, had grown apart from the mother tongue.

In 1806, Webster published *A Compendious Dictionary of the English Language.* By *compendious,* he meant "concise, brief, a summary." Like many writers of his day, however, Webster never used a short, clear word where a long, hard one would do. And like most dictionary makers, he was fond of elegant, obscure words.

Webster's dictionary is important in our story for a good reason, however. In the long history of lexicography, it showed for the first time how Americans spoke English. Of the 37,000 words in Webster's dictionary, about 5,000 were native to America and never before had appeared in an English dictionary. *Squash, skunk, raccoon, hickory, caucus, presidency, congressional, applesauce,* and *bullfrog* are examples.

Like Johnson, Webster searched for words in books, but he also tried something new—and established a principle of dictionary making that has been followed ever since. He began recording words as he heard people use them. In doing so, he followed Johnson's theory that spoken words make up a language.

Unlike Johnson, though, Webster had no ideas about fixing the language. Language, he said, was something fluid, ever changing. But the schoolmaster in him had a few ideas about fixing the spelling of some words. The way many words were spelled, he noted, had no relation to the way they were pronounced. This offended Webster's neat and orderly way of doing things.

Therefore, as he went about writing the *Compendious,* he changed the spelling of many words to match their sound. He dropped the silent *u* in the English spelling of *honour* and *favour* and wrote *honor* and *favor,* and the final *k* in *musick, logick,* and *publick* and used instead *music, logic,* and *public.* He also dropped the second *l* in *traveller, labelled,* and *farewell* and transposed the last two letters in English words like *centre* and *theatre.*

He also tried to simplify the spelling of other words by dropping silent letters—*e* from *imagine, e* from *definite, b* from *thumb, a* from *feather,* and *a* from *head.* For these spellings, he substituted *imagin, definit, thum, fether,* and *hed.*

When Webster's brother-in-law saw these newly minted words in the *Compendious,* he dashed off a quick letter: "I ain't quite ripe yet for your spelling." Most people agreed.

For some mysterious reasons, Americans two hundred years ago went along with *favor, honor, public, logic, music, traveler,* and *labeled.* They also agreed to switch the *re* to *er* in *center* and *theater.* But they objected strongly to most of the other changes Webster suggested. We still write *thumb* with a *b, head* and *feather* with an *a, farewell* with a double *l,* and *imagine* and *definite* with a final *e* even though these letters serve no purpose— except perhaps to show the unpredictable way language develops and that people, not grammarians or dictionary makers, determine how we spell the words we read and write.

The *Compendious* sold well, but it was only a warm-up for Webster's next project, *An American Dictionary of the English*

Language, a task to which he devoted his days for the next twenty-two years.

One day a traveler from Scotland stopped at Webster's home. Captain Basil Hall found the aging lexicographer in his orderly study. As usual, he was wearing black knee breeches and black silk stockings. All his books were neatly arranged on shelves, all papers carefully stacked. Why, Captain Hall asked, was Webster working on yet another dictionary?

Like most scholars absorbed in their work, Webster didn't tolerate interruptions gracefully. His tone was frosty. "And why not?"

'Because there are words enough already!" retorted Captain Hall and left.

Webster had an expert's scorn for the opinions of people like Captain Hall about his work—and for good reason. He probably knew more about languages than any other person in the world at that time. But Hall's ignorant criticism was a sign of what was in store for Webster's new work.

Webster finished his great dictionary in 1828. He was an old man now of seventy years. In his diary, he described his feelings:

"When I had come to the last word, I was seized with a trembling, which made it somewhat difficult to hold my pen steady for writing. The cause seems to have been the thought that I might not then live to finish the work. . . . But I summoned strength to finish the last word, and then walking about the room for a few minutes, I recovered."

The last word was *zygomatic.*

An American Dictionary of the English Language came out in two volumes with 70,000 words. It carried 12,000 American words not in Johnson's dictionary.

In his new work, Webster included words simply because people used them—something new at the time, but a principle of dictionary making ever since. He included Indian words that newer Americans had adopted for themselves, like *opossum* and *raccoon,* and words used by farmers and slaves, like *banjo* and *hominy.*

The words are familiar to us—we would expect to find them in a dictionary—but 150 years ago they caused an immediate uproar.

A newspaper, the Boston *Palladium*, called them "low" words. Webster's new dictionary was a "folly," the editor wrote, "because a language at its zenith, like ours, and expressive in the extreme, requires no introduction of new words."

"Foul and unclean things!" another newspaper said of the words used by slaves. It labeled Webster's masterpiece "Noah's Ark!"

The stings of his critics hurt Webster, but the old scholar replied gravely: "It is quite impossible to stop the progress of language. Words and expressions will be forced into use in spite of the objections of newspaper writers."

With his second dictionary, Webster also continued his efforts to change the spelling of many words—a rigid streak in his otherwise progressive attitude toward words: *ake* for *ache, wimin* for *women, tung* for *tongue, soop* for *soup, wo* for *who, cloke* for *cloak. Deaf,* he insisted, should be pronounced to rhyme with *leaf,* and not sound like the more common *def.*

Unlike his speller and first dictionary, though, Webster's two-volume dictionary did not sell well. Its $15 price was more than people wanted to pay for a dictionary.

But this didn't trouble the independent Webster. Despite advanced age and dwindling funds, he started on yet a third dictionary. For another twelve years, working alone in his study, he revised his two-volume work.

In his third dictionary, he gave in to his critics on one small point. He changed the spelling of words that people objected to, not because he thought their spelling correct and his wrong, but simply because he felt a dictionary should mirror the language as people used it and not as a dictionary maker would like to see it used.

In 1840, Webster finished his last dictionary. It carried 5,000 more words than his 1828 edition. But he couldn't find a publisher for his work. So, ever independent, ever walking his own path, he borrowed money from a bank, found a printer, and published it himself. He placed a price of $15 on his dictionary, but again people wouldn't pay it.

Bankrupt and on his death bed three years later, the old wordsmith suddenly sat up, told his grown children that a "crepuscule" was falling over him, settled back on his pillow, and died. He might have said "twilight," but he chose instead to pay a final loving tribute to special words.

Webster's children faced the problem of what to do with the unsold copies of his last dictionary and how to pay off the printer, George and Charles Merriam of Springfield, Massachusetts.

The debt was paid off when the Merriam brothers bought the dictionary and legalized the name Merriam-Webster. They neglected, however, to legalize the single name Webster. Today, if a company wants to publish a dictionary and use the name Webster in the title, it can do so. The name can be used by anyone. But the G. & C. Merriam Company, publisher of the Merriam-Webster dictionaries, is the only company today that continues Noah Webster's work.

On September 24, 1847, the two Merriam brothers brought out the first Merriam-Webster dictionary. Since that year, the company has published new editions, as the language grew and changed, in 1864, 1890, 1909, and 1934.

In 1961, the company published *Webster's Third New International Dictionary of the English Language, Unabridged.* The language had grown enormously since Webster's day. The last word of the 450,000 words in this massive volume is *zyzzogeton,* 70 more *z* words after *zygomatic,* the word that closed Webster's great 1828 volume. It was the kind of word that would have delighted the old wordsmith.

Chapter Five

The Greatest Dictionary
of All

Johnson's and Webster's dictionaries recorded words used by people in England and America during their lifetimes. Then, in 1857, an Irish Archbishop, Dean Richard Trench, came up with an idea for a remarkable new dictionary, a dictionary of the entire English language, a record—or biography—of each word for as long as people kept written records. This new dictionary, Dean Trench said, would draw "a sweep-net over the whole extent of English literature."

Neither Dean Trench nor anyone else really understood the length of time or the gigantic amount of work such a dictionary would require. And maybe it was just as well they didn't. If they had, the project would most certainly have never been started.

Work on what was to become *The Oxford English Dictionary* began at Oxford University in England. A group of volunteer readers—all people interested in the project but unpaid—met one day and began dipping into books, old records, and handwritten manuscripts produced before the printing press was invented. These volunteers began writing down sentences to record the way words were used as far back as the early English Bible and the reign of Alfred the Great (849-899).

For the next twenty years, the work progressed in a rather haphazard manner. By the end of the 1870s, though, the project desperately needed organization, and in 1879 Sir James A. H. Murray became the first of four editors.

In the garden of his home, Sir James built a corrugated iron shed—the "Scriptorium." With the help of two daughters and three assistant editors, he began organizing the twenty-year collection of word notes into 1,029 pigeonholes.

By now, two thousand volunteer readers from all over the world were sending in words. Some readers kept at the work for over fifty years. The record number of quotations sent in by a reader was 165,000.

Five years later, in 1884, the first volume, A-B, of *The Oxford English Dictionary* was ready for the printer. The first volume had taken twenty-seven years to produce. When Sir James was asked how long it would take to work through the alphabet to Z and publish the final volume, the old man thoughtfully stroked his full white beard and confidently replied, "Eleven years!"

Sir James misjudged by thirty-three years. By 1915, the staff had worked through T and, in 1928—seventy-one years after Dean Trench had thought of the idea—the tenth and final volume, X-Y-Z, was published. (During this period, the Panama Canal was dug, but it took only ten years, 1904–1914, to complete.) The staff observed the event by presenting a set to the King of England, George V, and to the President of the United States, Calvin Coolidge. Some of the people associated with the dictionary had worked on it for as long as fifty years. The same man who had set the type for the first volume in 1884 was still setting type for the last volume, a service of over forty-four years.

But even after three-quarters of a century of writing the OED, the staff decided that it still was not finished. No sooner was the complete set made available to bookstores for sale than the staff began to update the work by preparing a new edition. The new edition included words that had entered the language since the first volume was published.

In 1933, the revised edition of the OED was published. It required 13 volumes, contained 414,825 definitions in 16,569 pages, and weighed 105 pounds. "There is no dictionary in the world to compare with it," a London newspaper wrote.

Animals

hen   rooster   chickens

goose   geese   turkey

pony   ponies

17

A picture dictionary—pictures with labels—of 524 words; for boys and girls in kindergarten and first grade. (From *Thorndike-Barnhart My Pictionary,* © 1970 by Scott, Foresman and Company)

A page from an 800-word dictionary for first graders. Sentences illustrate different forms of a word. (From *Thorndike-Barnhart My First Picture Dictionary,* © 1970 by Scott, Foresman and Company)

What We Do

bend
The strong man is bending an iron bar. He bent one until it broke. He has bent many bars.

bite
George was biting an apple. He bit his finger by mistake. He has bitten two fingers.

blow
Jim is blowing his horn. Bill blew his horn first. All the boys have blown their horns.

bounce
The boy is bouncing the ball. He bounced it high.

51

bet say you will give something to someone if he is right and you are wrong: *He bet that he could beat me to the corner. I have bet that he couldn't.* **bet** or **bet ted, bet ting.**

bet ter 1. more than good: *This cake is good, but that cake is better.* See **good.** 2. in a more than good way: *He sang that song well, but he sang this one better.* See **well.**

be tween in the space or time from one thing to another: *There is a rock between two trees. We'll be home between two and three o'clock.*

be yond 1. farther away: *Look beyond the fence for your ball.* 2. farther than: *Don't go beyond the corner.*

bib 1. a cloth worn under the chin by a baby. 2. the top part of an apron. See the picture. **bibs.**

Bi ble a holy book. **Bi bles.**

bi cy cle a vehicle with two wheels, one behind the other. You ride it by pushing two pedals. **bi cy cles.**

big 1. much in size or many in amount: *a big dog, a big class.* 2. grown up: *a big girl.* 3. important: *big news.* **big ger, big gest.**

bike a bicycle. **bikes.**

bill¹ 1. an account of how much money a person owes someone: *Send me a bill for what I bought.* 2. a piece of paper money: *a dollar bill.* **bills.**

bill² the mouth of a bird. See the picture. **bills.**

bin a box or place shut in on all sides, for holding such things as grain and coal. See the picture. **bins.**

bind 1. tie together; hold together; fasten: *Bind the package with string.* 2. wrap a wound: *The doctor will bind your wound.* **bound, bind ing.**

bet

bind

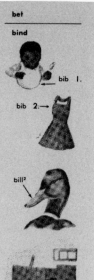

bib 1.

bib 2.—➤

bill²

coal bin

25

A page from a 4,089-word dictionary for second graders. Guide words (*bet* / *bind*) appear at the top of the page. Other features: divided entry words for writing; tenses of verbs; plurals of nouns. Definitions include illustrative sentences. (From *Thorndike-Barnhart My Second Picture Dictionary,* © 1971 by Scott, Foresman and Company)

This dictionary for third and fourth graders presents 26,140 entries. It also offers etymologies—word origins and history—idioms, and a short pronunciation key at the top of the page. (From *Thorndike-Barnhart Beginning Dictionary,* © 1974 by Scott, Foresman and Company)

D d

hat, āge, fär; let, ēqual, tėrm; it, ice;
hot, ōpen, ôrder; oil, out; cup, put, rüle; ch, child;
ng, long; sh, she; th, thin; ʈʜ, then; zh, measure;

ə represents *a* in about,
e in taken, *i* in pencil, *o* in lemon, *u* in circus.

D or **d** (dē), the fourth letter of the alphabet. There are two *d*'s in *dead. noun, plural D's or d's.*

dab (dab), 1 touch lightly; tap: *Mother dabbed her face with a powder puff.* 2 a pat or tap: *The cat made a dab at the butterfly.* 3 a small, soft or moist mass: *dabs of butter.* 4 a little bit: *Put a dab of paint on this spot you missed.* 1 *verb,* **dabbed, dab bing;** 2-4. *noun.*

dab ble (dab′əl), 1 dip in and out of water; splash: *We sat and dabbled our feet in the pool.* 2 work at a little: *He dabbled at painting but soon gave it up.* *verb,* **dab bled, dab bling.**

dachshund—5 to 9 inches high at the shoulder

dachs hund (däks′hunt′), a small dog with a long body and very short legs. *noun.* [from the German word *Dachshund,* formed from the words *Dachs,* meaning "badger," and *Hund,* meaning "dog." The breed was developed for hunting badgers.]

dad (dad), father. *noun.*

dad dy (dad′ē), father. *noun, plural* **dad dies.**

daddy-longlegs
about life size

dad dy-long legs (dad′ē lông′legz′), animal that looks much like a spider, but does not bite. It has a small body and long, thin legs. *noun, plural* **dad dy-long legs.**

daf fo dil (daf′ə dil), plant with long, slender leaves and yellow or white flowers that bloom in the spring. *noun.*

daft (daft), 1 silly; foolish. 2 crazy. *adjective.*

dag ger (dag′ər), a small weapon with a short, pointed blade, used for stabbing. *noun.*

dai ly (dā′lē), 1 done, happening, or appearing every day: *a daily visit, a daily paper.* 2 every day; day by day: *The bus runs daily.* 3 newspaper printed every day. 1 *adjective,* 2 *adverb,* 3 *noun, plural* **dai lies.**

dain ti ly (dān′tl ē), in a dainty way. *adverb.*

dain ty (dān′tē), 1 fresh, delicate, and pretty: *The violet is a dainty spring flower.* 2 delicate in tastes and feeling: *She is dainty about her eating, never spilling or taking big bites.* 3 good to eat; delicious: *"Wasn't that a dainty dish to set before the king?"* 4 something very good to eat: *Candy and nuts are dainties.* 1-3 *adjective,* **dain ti er, dain ti est;** 4 *noun, plural* **dain ties.**

dair y (der′ē), 1 farm where milk and cream are produced and butter and cheese made. 2 store or company that sells milk, cream, butter, and cheese. 3 room or building where milk and cream are kept and made into butter and cheese. *noun, plural* **dair ies.** [from the earlier English word *deyerie,* from the old English word *dæge,* meaning "kneader of bread." Later on, the word was used to mean "workers in a milking room."]

da is (dā′is), a raised platform at one end of a hall or large room. A throne, seats of honor, or a desk may be set on a dais. *noun, plural* **da is es.**

dai sy (dā′zē), a wild flower having white, pink, or yellow petals around a yellow center. *noun, plural* **dai sies.** [from the old English phrase *dæges eage,* meaning "day's eye," because the petals open in the morning and close in the evening]

dale (dāl), valley. *noun.*

dal ly (dal′ē), 1 act in a playful manner: *The spring breeze dallies with the flowers.* 2 flirt with danger, temptation, or a person; trifle: *He dallied with the offer for days, but finally refused it.* 3 linger idly; loiter: *He was late because he dallied along the way.* 4 waste (time): *He dallied the afternoon away looking out the window and daydreaming.* *verb,* **dal lied, dal ly ing.**

daffodil

frigate (def. 1)

fringe (def. 1)
two styles

frieze

342

For students in grades five, six, seven, and eight, this dictionary contains 56,700 entries. It lists proper nouns that students come upon in their reading, introduces maps, gives multiple meanings for many words (e.g., *horse* has seven meanings), and supplies usage notes. (From *Thorndike-Barnhart Intermediate Dictionary,* Second edition, © 1974 by Scott, Foresman and Company)

wigwag (def. 1)

wigwam

A page from a high school dictionary containing 95,000 entries that reflects current social trends, scientific advances, and contemporary personalities. Synonyms help students distinguish between words of related meanings. More definitions for individual words are also included— e.g., *stock* has 37 definitions compared with 19 in a dictionary for junior high students. (From *Thorndike-Barnhart Advanced Dictionary,* Second edition, © 1974 by Scott, Foresman and Company)

Samuel Johnson (1709-1784) created the modern English dictionary. A friend described him as "tall, stout, grand, and authoritative, but he stoops horribly, his back is quite round." This is the unfinished "Barry portrait" of the great lexicographer. (Culver Pictures)

The title page to Johnson's *A Dictionary of the English Language*. In the Preface, Johnson wrote: "Every language . . . has its improprieties and absurdities which it is the duty of the lexicographer to correct. . . . This is my idea of an English Dictionary . . ." (Rare Book Division, The New York Public Library, Astor, Lenox and Tilden Foundations)

A

DICTIONARY

OF THE

ENGLISH LANGUAGE:

IN WHICH

The WORDS are deduced from their ORIGINALS,

AND

ILLUSTRATED in their DIFFERENT SIGNIFICATIONS

BY

EXAMPLES from the beſt WRITERS.

TO WHICH ARE PREFIXED,

A HISTORY of the LANGUAGE,

AND

An ENGLISH GRAMMAR.

By SAMUEL JOHNSON, A.M.

In TWO VOLUMES.

VOL. I.

Cum tabulis animum cenſoris fumet honeſti :
Audebit quæcunque parum ſplendoris habebunt,
Et fine pondere erunt, et honore indigna ferentur,
Verba movere loco ; quamvis invita recedant,
Et verſentur adhuc intra penetralia Veſtæ :
Obſcurata diu populo bonus eruet, atque
Proferet in lucem ſpeciofa vocabula rerum,
Quæ priſcis memorata Catonibus atque Cethegis,
Nunc ſitus informis premit et deſerta vetuſtas.   HOR.

LONDON,

Printed by W. STRAHAN,

For J. and P. KNAPTON ; T. and T. LONGMAN ; C. HITCH and L. HAWES ;
A. MILLAR ; and R. and J. DODSLEY.

MDCCLV.

A tough, dedicated, self-taught scholar, Noah Webster (1758-1843) created America's first dictionary. Where dictionary making was concerned, he admitted no error—probably because he knew more about language (and more languages: 26) than any other person of his day. (G. & C. Merriam Company)

A page from Webster's copy of Johnson's *A Dictionary of the English Language*. The notes are Webster's. In the right margin, he disagreed with Johnson's definition of "toot" as a verb—"To pry; to peep; to search narrowly . . ." Webster's note reads: "No—to make a noise . . . to hoot or howl." (Rare Book Division, The New York Public Library, Astor, Lenox and Tilden Foundations)

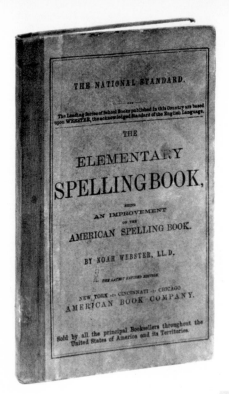

As a young man, Webster wrote this grammar-speller-reader, the first used in America's schools. Earnings from the sales of millions of copies supported Webster and allowed him time to write dictionaries. (G. & C. Merriam Company)

The title page to *A Compendious Dictionary of the English Language* published in 1806. Today's Merriam-Webster dictionaries are direct descendants of this dictionary, Webster's—and America's—first. (G. & C. Merriam Company)

A

Compendious Dictionary

OF THE

English Language.

In which FIVE THOUSAND Words are added to the number found in the BEST ENGLISH COMPENDS;

The ORTHOGRAPHY is, in some instances, corrected;

The PRONUNCIATION marked by an Accent or other suitable Direction;

And the DEFINITIONS of many Words amended and improved.

TO WHICH ARE ADDED FOR THE BENEFIT OF THE

MERCHANT, the STUDENT and the TRAVELLER,

I.——TABLES of the MONEYS of most of the commercial Nations in the world, with the value expressed in Sterling and Cents.

II.——TABLES of WEIGHTS and MEASURES, ancient and modern, with the proportion between the several weights used in the principal cities of Europe.

III.——The DIVISIONS of TIME among the Jews, Greeks and Romans, with a Table exhibiting the Roman manner of dating.

IV.——An official List of the POST-OFFICES in the UNITED STATES, with the States and Counties in which they are respectively situated and the distance of each from the seat of Government.

V.——The NUMBER of INHABITANTS in the United States, with the amount of EXPORTS.

IV.——New and interesting CHRONOLOGICAL TABLES of remarkable Events and Discoveries.

By NOAH WEBSTER, Esq.

From Sidney's Press.

FOR HUDSON & GOODWIN, BOOK-SELLERS, HARTFORD, AND INCREASE COOKE & CO. BOOK-SELLERS, NEW-HAVEN.

1806.

GEORGE MERRIAM   CHARLES MERRIAM

George and Charles Merriam printed Webster's 1840 dictionary in this shop at the corner of Main and State Streets in Springfield, Massachusetts. The brothers also sold books and stationery. Today, the G. & C. Merriam Company is still located in Springfield, but in a newer, larger building. (G. & C. Merriam Company)

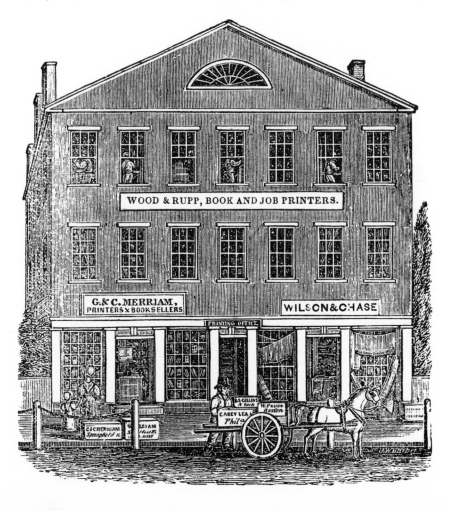

Dean Richard Trench whose idea of drawing "a sweep-net" over English literature created the greatest of all English-language dictionaries, *The Oxford English Dictionary*. (Culver Pictures)

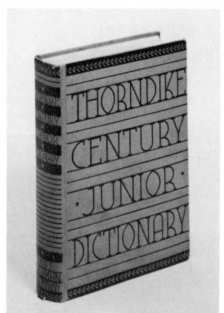

Edward L. Thorndike, creator of the first dictionary for children. (Teachers College, Columbia University)

The first dictionary for children, the *Thorndike-Century Junior Dictionary,* was published in 1935. (Scott, Foresman and Company)

Paging through the volumes shows what a tremendous work of scholarship the OED is.

The word *set* requires 23 pages to define and has 213 different meanings.

The definition for *go* fills nearly 12 pages.

Get requires 22 columns—7⅓ pages—and has 76 different meanings.

Take offers 103 definitions on 14 pages. The complete definition requires just 5 inches over 33 feet to present. (A modern unabridged dictionary, by contrast, uses about three feet to define *take*. A college dictionary uses one foot.)

"These mighty volumes are more than a dictionary," one scholar said. "They are the mellow history of the English language."

Besides offering definitions of words, each word is illustrated by quotations from many authors, at least one per century, showing how the word has been used since it first began. The meaning of each word, in each of its senses, is made clear from the quotations.

"Tracing each word down through the centuries," said one worker, "can become an addiction. In its earliest use, by the way, *addiction* meant 'a surrender or dedication of anyone to a master.' Samuel Johnson first used the word as a synonym for habit in 'an addiction to tobacco.'"

The OED notes how words like *addiction* have changed meaning over hundreds of years. Nearly six hundred years ago, church people called the Virgin Mary "silly." At that time, *silly* meant "blessed." Gradually the word changed meaning. It went through "defenseless" and only recently became a synonym for "foolish."

Badminton was originally the name of the Duke of Beaufort's country home. Then, in 1853, it became the name of a "cooling summer drink . . . of mingled claret, sugar, and soda water." By 1874, it was used as the name for a game "resembling lawn-tennis," played with a net, rackets, and shuttlecocks instead of balls.

The OED records the life of words—how they are born and how they grow. It also records how some words die. *Ignotism* once meant "a mistake due to ignorance." It last appeared in an English magazine in 1737. ("It has 92 Errors or Ignotisms in it.") Back in Samuel Johnson's day, *gome* was the black grease used on the axle of a cart wheel. Today, we no longer use *gome* or *ignotism.*

As if the original edition of the OED was not extraordinary enough, a new edition appeared in 1971 that was even more remarkable. Through a process of photographic reduction, the original 13 volumes were reduced to two volumes of 2,048 pages (A-O) and 2,068 pages (P-Z). Four pages of the original edition appear on each page of *The Compact Edition of The Oxford English Dictionary.* With the two volumes—weighing 17 pounds—comes a magnifying glass so people can easily read the reduced-in-size print.

In 1972, yet another edition of the OED made its appearance, *A Supplement to The Oxford English Dictionary,* Vol. I, A-G, 1331 pages. Vol. II (H-P) and Vol. III (Q-Z) are now in the works and scheduled for publication in the next few years.

To find words that have appeared in English since earlier editions of the OED, one hundred readers from all over the world scour books, newspapers, magazines, and printed material of all kinds. The new edition quotes England's Queen Elizabeth II, for example, using *butterflies* in the sense of anxiety: "I always have butterflies when I open Parliament."

The new edition also includes new U.S. words like *Frisbee,* the plastic flying saucer that adults and children alike enjoy playing with. For the origin of the word, it states that the Frisbee was invented by a Los Angeles building inspector who was inspired by the flights of pie tins used by the Frisbie bakery in Bridgeport, Connecticut.

Slang words that have become a permanent part of the language also appear in the supplement. The British word *gazoomph* means the practice in England by some real estate agents of suddenly hiking the price of a house or land as a buyer is about to sign a contract to purchase it. The last word in the first volume is *gyver*—Australian and New Zealand slang meaning "affectation of speech or behavior, especially in the phrase 'to put on the gyver!'"

The Oxford English Dictionary will probably never be duplicated. In dictionary making, it is the equivalent to what in science would be man's landing on the moon and, in art, the *Mona Lisa.* Dean Trench's idea for a "sweep-net" dictionary became the single most valuable piece of scholarship in the English language.

Chapter Six

Where Do All
the Words in the Dictionary
Come From?

How many words are in the English language?

When George Washington became our first President, there were about 100,000. Today, dictionary makers guess the number to be anywhere from 450,000 to 3,000,000.

But the truth is, no one really knows. Because our language changes so rapidly—new words coming into use almost daily, old words that have outlived their usefulness dropping out—an accurate count is impossible to make.

What language experts—called philologists—do know, though, is where the words that make up English come from and how our language started.

One finding philologists have made may surprise you. The English language—the words we speak, read, and write—is actually made up of words from a variety of other languages: French, German, Arabic, Swedish, Dutch, Persian, Greek, Chinese, Portuguese, Latin, and just about any other language you can name including Hindi and Bengali.

English is really a melting pot of many languages. Even some of the most primitive people on earth—spear-carrying aborigines from central Australia who live today much as they did in the Stone Age—have contributed words to our language. This grand mixture of words from all the world's languages, including a massive injection of original American words, has made English the most expressive tongue spoken by any people today.

Philologists have written volumes about the English language and how it grew. The subject is vast and complicated. For our purposes, though, we'll stick to one aspect of the subject: the dozens of little word trickles that over centuries have come together into the living stream of the language we use today.

The Beginnings in England

England, wrote Sir Winston Churchill, is an island "so tilted that its mountains lie all to the west and north, while south and east is a gently undulating landscape of valleys, open downs and slow rivers. It is very accessible to the invader."

The first invaders of England were tribes of wanderers from central Europe called Celts. About five hundred years before the birth of Christ, these tall, fair-haired, and hardy people crossed the English Channel and settled in England. Not much is known about the Celts, and only a few words—a dozen or so—from their language remain in English today: *bog, glen, whiskey, bin, crag, bug, kick, creak, basket, dagger, lad.*

The Celtic word *cumb*—meaning "deep valley"—survives today in the names of English villages like Duncombe and Winchcombe. Bryn Mawr, the name of one of our famous colleges, is a Celtic word. *Bryn* means "hill"; *mawr* means "great."

A second invasion of England took place in 55 B.C. when the Roman general Julius Caesar led shiploads of soldiers to the green island and easily conquered the peaceful Celts.

The Romans stayed four hundred years. They built towns, temples, large country homes, and some of the finest paved roads the ancient world knew.

The Romans spoke Latin. The Roman name for the numerous forts or camps they built was *castra.* All towns in England today whose names end in *chester, caster,* or *cester*—Portchester, Westchester, Worcester, Lancaster—were built on the sites of the original Roman camps.

By 410 A.D., however, the Romans were having trouble at home.

Barbarians from northern Europe were attacking Rome, and Emperor Honorius called his army home from England.

As the Roman legions marched to the beaches to board their ships, the Celtic leader, Vortigern, realized that his people were now open to attack by the savage Picts and Scots from the mountains of Scotland and Ireland. He appealed to the Roman emperor for protection. Honorius sent back the following chilling reply: "The cantons [Roman occupied lands] should take steps to defend themselves." The statement amounted to a death sentence for the peaceful Celts.

No sooner had the last Roman soldier left than the Picts and Scots attacked. Defenseless, Vortigern appealed for help to the Jutes, a tribe across the English Channel. He offered free land and money in return for protection against the Picts and Scots. The bargain cost the Celtic chief his life.

The Jutes defeated the Picts and Scots, but unfortunately their chief liked the fertile land and decided to stay. He killed off Vortigern and his court and set up his own rule.

The Jutes, however, were not left with their victory for long. Other tribes from across the channel invaded the green island, the Saxons in 477 and the Angles in 547. The Angles became the dominant tribe, and by the year 700 the island was called Angleland. The language became known as Englisc and the people were called Angelcynn—kin of the Angles.

The Anglo-Saxons were hunters, farmers, and fishers. They led a close family life. Most of their words were short one- and two-syllable words that reflected their daily occupations: *ax, tool, farm, shield, field, sword, bread, man, woman, father, mother, brother, sister, child, food, sleep, house.* About 50,000 Anglo-Saxon words remain in English today.

In the eighth and ninth centuries, other tribes invaded England. From across the North Sea, from the cold fjords of Norway and Sweden, came ruthless raiders called Vikings. In fleets of 300 to 400 ships, each 70 feet long and propelled by 15 oars on a side, ships like the "Great Dragon" and "Long Serpent" bore the invaders up the broad rivers leading to the interior. In 793, after a Viking band had raided a monastery at Lindisfarne, slaying unarmed monks and plundering the library, a survivor wrote, "Never before has such a terror appeared in Britain."

The Vikings stayed in armed camps, then brought over their wives and children and formed settlements. The first generation of Viking warriors produced a second generation of farmers and craftsmen who intermarried with the Angelcynns.

Most words we use today with *sh* and *sk* sounds are Viking in origin: *disc* became *dish; fisc, fish; scip, ship; biscop, bishop.* Other Viking words entered English without change: *scrape, scrub, skill, skin, bask, whisk, sky, skill, skirt.*

About 1,400 towns and villages in England today retain names of Viking origin: Woodthorp, Althorp, Linthorp. *Thorp* was the Viking word for village. Another Viking word, *toft*—meaning "a piece of ground"—survives today in other place names: Brimtoft, Mapletoft, Nortoft.

Despite the introduction of new words, however, the Anglo-Saxon language remained dominant. By the year 1,000, the island was called Englaland, the language Anglish.

The Last Invasion

On September 28, 1066, William of Normandy sailed from France with his army and in a little over two short weeks conquered the English. On Christmas Day in Westminster Abbey, he crowned himself William the Conqueror, King of England. William was England's last invader.

William's language, French, became the language of the ruling class. The French became the chief landowners and the officials of the church and government. French was also taught in schools.

But the common people who dealt with the French ruling class —the shopowners, craftsmen, and tradesmen—adopted French only as a second language. With each other, they continued to speak English.

Over the next three hundred years, English absorbed many French words: *air, army, art, blue, color, chair, dinner, judge, justice, mayor, paper, prison, towel, aunt, uncle, niece, nephew, cousin, boil, cash, charge, cost, expense, price, crown, nation, beef, veal, bacon, fry.*

We also have the French to thank for the silent *ue* in *tongue* and the silent *u* in *guilt, build,* and *guess.* Anglo-Saxon was a much more practical language. It simply spelled words as they sounded: *tung, gilt, bilt, ges.* Somehow, though, the silent *ue* and *u* stayed in the language to confuse generations of students ever since.

The sixteenth and seventeenth centuries saw many new words enter the language. Shakespeare alone added 5,000: *courtship, hot-blooded, leapfrog, excellent, laughable, green-eyed.*

The most famous hangman in England—Derick—hanged so many lawbreakers at Tyburn that his name came to mean a device or framework—a *derrick*—for hoisting heavy objects.

English explorers like Sir Francis Drake visited foreign countries and returned to England with new words for the language: *igloo, banana.* From China came *tea;* from Arabia, *candy.*

Captain James Cook, exploring the Pacific Ocean in the *Endeavor,* discovered the east coast of Australia. In his diary for June 24, 1770, he described a long-tailed, high-jumping animal. The natives, he wrote, called it a "kangaroo." Another word he brought back described a curved piece of wood that, when thrown, circled through the air and returned to the thrower. Natives called it a "boomerang."

Thus did two more words, used by some of the most primitive people on earth, enter the great melting pot of the English language.

American English

The first American words to enter English were Indian. Early settlers in this country had no words to describe the many birds, animals, and growing things they had never seen before, so they used the same terms the Indians used. Today, we still use about 1,700 Indian words in everyday speech: *moose, moccasin, wigwam, chocolate, potato* are a few.

As settlers came to America, they also contributed words from their own language to English.

Early French settlers gave us *chowder, gopher, portage, prairie, toboggan.*

German settlers: *noodle, pretzel, sauerkraut.*

Dutch settlers: *boss, coleslaw, cookie, cranberry, dumb, pit, Santa Claus, spook, stoop, brandy, golf, wagon.*

With the opening of the west, Spanish and Mexican settlers brought in *canyon, bonanza, plaza, bronco, cinch, lasso, ranch, cockroach, tornado, alligator, cargo, mosquito, rodeo, vanilla.*

And Americans who traveled west to stake out the new country added *covered wagon, buckboard, backwater, homestretch, hired hand.*

President Thomas Jefferson made a *swivel chair* and contributed that word to the growing language. Benjamin Franklin, besides being a statesman, was also an inventor. He gave us *bifocals* and the *Franklin stove.*

In the eighteenth and nineteenth centuries, other inventors introduced the *cotton gin, telegraph, telephone, sewing machine, elevator, escalator, refrigerator,* and *skyscraper.* Adolphe Sax invented the *saxophone,* Rudolf Diesel the *diesel engine,* George Pullman a railroad sleeping car called the *pullman,* and Gabriel Fahrenheit gave his last name to a formula for measuring temperature.

Perhaps the greatest injection of new words into American English, though, came from the immigrants, the hordes of people from other countries who came to live in America in the late nineteenth and early twentieth centuries. Here is a sampling of words we use every day that were originally used in other languages:

Food and eating: *supper, menu, lettuce, salad, dessert* were all originally French. *Macaroni,* Italian. *Cheese,* Latin. *Tomato,* Mexican. *Coffee*, Turkish. *Cocoa*, Spanish. *Tapioca*, South American Indian. *Yams*, Portuguese. *Goulash*, Hungarian.

Clothing: *jacket*, French. *Trousers*, Irish. *Shawl*, Persian. *Pajamas*, Hindi.

Music: *trombone, violin, piano, opera,* and most of our musical terms are Italian in origin. *Waltz* is German. *Polka*, Czech. *Tango*, Spanish. *Trumpet* and *bugle*, French.

The flow of words from other languages into English has never stopped.

From Arabic, we get *algebra, cork, magazine, zero*.

Italian: *balcony, colonel, model, umbrella*.

Persian: *checkers, lemon, lilac, paradise, spinach*.

Greek: *acrobat, Bible, cheer, cyclone, idiot, magic, elastic, democracy, grammar, biography, rhythm, orchestra, biology, astronomy, television, phonograph*.

Hindi: *bungalow*.

Bengali: *dinghy*.

Abracadabra comes from the Aramaic *abhadda kedabrah*—"vanish at this word."

So long comes from the Arabic *salaam*—"peace."

Hey Ba-Ba Re-Bop

Another type of word that enriches English is slang. Slang is generally defined as "below the standard of cultivated speech . . . characterized by raciness . . . jargon of a particular class or group." However, slang does much to flavor a language, to make it gayer and more colorful.

We think of slang as being new words or fresh uses of old words. But there is nothing new about slang itself. Every generation develops its own special expressions. In the 1860's in England, *gooseberry* meant "all that is dreary and old-fashioned." Your grandparents used *the cat's pajamas* and *twenty-three skiddoo*. Your parents may have used *Hey Ba-Ba Re-Bop* and *Beat me, Daddy, eight to the bar!*

Some slang words take on respectability with the passing of time. Shakespeare, for example, used slang frequently in his plays —*hubbub, fretful, dwindle, clumsy, bogus*—and today these words are quite proper. Other slang he invented is still considered slang: *beat it, done me wrong, fall for it, not so hot.*

An American slang expression that never made the jump to respectability is *bury the hatchet.* The Pilgrims took the original Indian term, translated it to English, and used it to mean "forget past differences."

Slang has a way of expressing in a word or phrase a whole blend of feelings. *Up tight* is a special and highly articulate way of expressing tension whether in the business office or classroom. *Out of sight* aptly describes something too splendid to describe.

Nor is slang used only by people under twenty-one. Adults, too, use and create slang, but instead of slang they call it jargon—"the special language of a group or class." The garbageman has become a *sanitation engineer.* Cemeteries are now *memorial parks* and prisons *houses of detention.* Slums are the *inner city* or *depressed areas.* Poor people are *underprivileged* and the crippled are *handicapped.* A space scientist, watching a moon rocket explode on the launch pad, described the failure as an *unsuccess.* Old people are *senior citizens.* ("Damn it!" roared one eighty-four-year-old man. "I am *not* a senior citizen! I am an old man!")

"Slang," said one language specialist, "has kept American English the marvelous, unpredictable, zany, and utterly useful language it is!"

Crackback and Folk Mass

Each year, thousands of new words enter the language. Since 1945, more words have entered English than in all the centuries since Shakespeare's day, almost four hundred years ago.

New developments in science brought in new words like *television, laser, UNIVAC, vinyl.*

America's space program added *countdown, reentry, A-OK, astronaut, nose cone, retro-rocket, splashdown.*

American business contributed *assembly line, payroll, trademark, trouble shooter, sit-down strike, fink, goon, scab, white-collar worker.*

The American people coined *carhop, double-talk, hot rod, jukebox, whirlybird, smog, drum majorette, motorcade, cookout, shopping center, freeway, hardtop, deep-freeze.*

When a dictionary comes out, it's possible to count the number of new words that have entered the language. Between the publication of the big Merriam-Webster unabridgeds, one in 1934 and the next in 1961, 100,000 words entered English. A few examples are *globalize, hatemonger, loyalty oath, segregated, gatecrasher, beatnik, boo-boo, yakety-yak, drip-dry,* and *litterbug.* Developments in chemistry alone added 17,000 of these words.

A new edition of a popular desk dictionary in the ten years between 1963 and 1973 showed 22,000 new words. During these years, our language was enriched by *bioinstrumentation* and *lunar excursion module* from space, *perfecta* and *crackback* from sports, *acid rock* and *folk mass* from music, *noise pollution* and *biodegradable* from ecology, and many more.

For 2,500 years, the English language has continued to grow. Daily, dictionary makers record the changes. The next chapter shows how they do it.

Chapter Seven

Making a
Modern Dictionary

Making a new dictionary is a massive and expensive publishing operation. A dictionary for the home or office carrying 150,000 words might cost four to five million dollars to produce. Printing 660,000 copies of one new dictionary like this required a strip of paper five feet wide and 18,000 miles long—a distance due east around the world from New York across Europe, Asia, and the Pacific Ocean to San Francisco. A big operation.

Because of the size of a new dictionary and the millions of type characters that go into its makeup, even periods and commas take on special importance. When the editors of *Webster's Third New International Dictionary, Unabridged,* decided to omit periods and commas after abbreviations in definitions—like adj., n., and v. (for adjective, noun, and verb)—they saved two million characters and 80 pages in each copy printed.

An unabridged dictionary will take five to ten years to produce. Besides definitions of words, it will include such extra features as an atlas, a foreign-language section (French, Spanish, German, and Italian of 30,000 words each), important events and dates in world history, and lists and tables of all kinds of useful information —air distances between selected cities, ocean deeps, national parks in the U.S. and Canada, waterfalls, rivers, and volcanoes of the world, colleges and universities, biographical names, geographical names, weights and measures, radio frequencies, chemical elements, and books of the Bible. (Mark Twain, author of *Tom*

Sawyer, once said of the dictonary, "I'm always surprised it knows so much!")

To gather this amount of information—and to insure its absolute accuracy—requires a staff of twenty-five to fifty dedicated editors, each of whom is a language expert, as well as a corps of outside consultants. A dictionary publisher estimated that to produce the massive *Webster's Third New International Dictionary, Un-abridged,* with its 2,662 pages and 450,000 vocabulary words would require one editor 757 years—in contrast to the eight years it took Samuel Johnson to write his dictionary. The *Random House Dictionary of the English Language* required eight years, an editorial staff of 45 people, and 350 consultants in 158 specialized fields to produce its 260,000 entry words in 2,059 pages.

Advising the editors on the accuracy of their definitions may be as many as 350 outside experts in 150 specialized fields—like Knots, Mosses and Liverworts, American History, and Zoology. Advising on sports, for example, might be the editors of a national sports magazine, on shipbuilding a retired captain in the merchant marine, on cooking the food editor of a large newspaper, on card playing a card game expert, on jazz a music writer for a large magazine. To check underworld slang, one dictionary publisher consulted a detective from the 40th Precinct of the New York Police Department.

The purpose of checking and rechecking words and definitions that go into a dictionary is to make it, one editor said, "as accurate a book as we could hope to make."

All this effort is well worth the time and money required to produce a new dictionary. Publishers of new dictionaries expect to make generous profits from their work. Every year, two-and-a-half-million dictionaries of every shape and size are sold in the United States alone. About 45,000 of these are the big unabridgeds. About one million are college or desk dictionaries used in homes and offices. The remainder are school dictionaries—for junior high school students down to kindergartners—and paperback dictionaries.

Making a modern dictionary is a complicated process. But it starts out in a very simple way, with 3 x 5 cards, the kind almost everyone uses to take notes on.

The Basic Tool

In New York a few years ago, a famous stage actress finished her second performance for the day. To a newspaper reporter in her dressing room, she said wearily, "Two shows a day drain a girl."

The next day, a dictionary editor noted the actress's use of the word *drain* in the story that the reporter wrote. Trained in languages, he saw that she had used the word in the sense of "exhaust." Up to this time, he knew that most people used drain to mean "to draw off gradually, as a liquid; to make empty or dry by drawing off a liquid." Because the actress had used *drain* in a new way, he jotted down the quotation on a citation slip.

A citation slip is the dictionary maker's basic tool for creating a new dictionary. A 3 x 5 card, it lists a word, the sentence in which it is used, the form of the word (verb, noun, adjective, etc.), the author's name, the publication in which the quotation appeared, and the page and column number and date.

For *drain*, the editor also added the abbreviation "fig." for "figuratively." This meant that *drain* had been used in an imaginative rather than an exact way.

In the same newspaper on the sports page, the editor found a new use for *puff*. "Hit too many homers," a baseball player was quoted as saying, "and people start puffing you up."

The player was using *puff* in the sense of "overrate," a shift of usage from "a gust of wind," "cloud puff," "pastry puff," or half a dozen other usages. Again the editor filled out a citation slip on this use of *puff*.

Besides scanning newspapers, editors spend a few hours each day reading magazines—all kinds, from fashion magazines to rocketry journals—as well as as cartoons, the Sears, Roebuck catalog, new books, restaurant menus, labels on cans and jars in supermarkets, ticket stubs, new traffic laws, toy assembly instructions, sports rule books. They also watch TV programs and listen to the radio, blank citation slips within reach to catch unusual pronunciations of words.

Each citation slip is carefully filed with all other citation slips on the same word. Banks of shallow drawers arranged alphabetically ("E to earth juice" might be the label on one drawer) hold the slips. About 850 slips fit in a drawer. In nearly two hundred years, the citation-slip files at the Merriam-Webster Company, Springfield, Massachusetts, have grown to over 12 million slips, the largest word bank in the world.

Editors add about 125,000 citation slips to the files each year. When all slips from various sources come together for any one word, then editors can see how people use a word in all its various forms.

Some words collect hundreds of citation slips. *Come* is one of the most thoroughly investigated of all words. Over 5,000 citation slips trace *come* back to the sixteenth century. Other words may be listed on only a single citation slip.

Before appearing in a dictionary, most words must be in use for at least five years and show up in print often enough to clearly establish their usage. "A new word deserves entry when evidence shows that it has been used frequently enough for us to know what it means and how it's used over a wide part of the country and that it has a strong likelihood of staying in the language," one editor said.

Rock 'n' roll appears in most new dictionaries today, but *rockabilly* does not. Editors decided that *rockabilly* was "ephemeral and omissible"—temporary and fit for leaving out—and thus didn't qualify.

Words like *rockabilly* that editors decide shouldn't be included in a new dictionary will be left in the citation files. Some words in a citation file will never appear in a dictionary; others will stay buried for years, then suddenly appear.

One citation slip stayed buried in a citation file for twenty-eight years before—in a single day actually—it became a term everyone knew and used. In January 1917, while reading a magazine called the *Yale Review*, an editor came across the following paragraph: "When you can drop just one atomic bomb and wipe out Paris or Berlin, war will have become monstrous and impossible. After the murder of women and babies from the air, it is no longer easy to believe that a mechanical device like the atomic bomb will keep men from fighting forevermore."

Without understanding the term, the editor snipped the paragraph out of the magazine and pasted it on a 3 x 5 card. He underlined *atomic bomb*, described it as "fanciful, a chemical explosion," and filed it away.

On August 6, 1945, the first atomic bomb used in warfare was dropped on Hiroshima, Japan, and newspapers around the world headlined the event. An editor, searching citation files to prepare a definition of the new term, found the original citation that had been filed twenty-eight years earlier. He used it to write a definition: "A bomb whose violent explosive power is due to the sudden release of atomic energy . . ."

Perhaps the fastest entry of a word into a dictionary happened in 1957. On October 4 of that year, the Russians sent the world's first satellite, Sputnik I, into orbit around the earth. An editor in New York saw the word in a newspaper delivered to his desk. He grabbed the phone and called a printing plant in the Midwest where his company's new dictionary was just about ready to be printed. "Stop the press!" he shouted. Over the long distance phone, he dictated a definition of the word. One day later, *sputnik* appeared in a dictionary and became part of the English language.

"The word," he said, "was used in English newspapers throughout the world. We didn't have to pile up evidence for it because millions of people saw it and began using it."

Slang expressions are new words, too, but editors always ponder long before deciding whether or not to include one in a dictionary. Because so many slang words appear briefly in speech and then disappear for good (called "nonce words"), some dictionary makers wait twenty-five years before including a new slang expression in print. Others rely on the number of citation slips a word gathers and on the variety of sources using a word. If only one magazine or newspaper uses a word, or if it is used in only one part of the country, it is not included in a dictionary. Not until a word piles up a significant number of citation slips and a dictionary editor senses that it has become a permanent part of the language is it given a place in the dictionary. *Corny, whodunit, mod,* and *getaway* are examples of recent slang words that have found their way into dictionaries.

But writing definitions involves more than just deciding how people use words. Writing definitions for many words requires careful fact-checking.

Over the three-quarters of a century in which it has published about thirty-five different dictionaries, Funk & Wagnalls (*Funk & Wagnalls Standard Dictionary; Funk & Wagnalls Comprehensive Standard International Dictionary*) has accumulated a library of thousands of fact-filled reference books, like encyclopedias, almanacs, atlases, and biographical dictionaries. Editors use these to check facts that go into many definitions. For example: Does an anteater have teeth (no) and does it eat anything besides ants? (Yes, termites.) What is the population of Santa Fe, New Mexico? (39,000.) When was President Andrew Jackson born? (1767.) What color is a cheetah's fur? (Black-spotted light brown to brownish orange.) How long is the Danube River in southeastern Europe and in what direction does it flow? (1,750 miles —generally eastward to the Black Sea.)

Readers want information like this when they look up a word. It's up to editors writing definitions to provide it and to make sure it's absolutely accurate—hence the checking in numerous reference books of any fact that goes into a definition.

"Deciding which new words will go into a dictionary, finding new words, writing definitions is a fine art," said a dictionary publisher. "To become a dictionary editor, you need a feeling for words. It's like musical talent—very hard to find. A dictionary editor needs *sprachgefühl*—that's German. There's no word in English that quite expresses the same quality. It means 'a sensitivity to language.' Which is one reason why, when we're looking for an editor, we don't run an ad in the want-ad section of the daily newspaper: 'Help wanted. Young man or woman to write dictionaries.' You never find one that way because what you're looking for is *sprachgefühl*."

He glanced out the window and stroked his chin. "*Sprachgefühl* —a great word to fill the mouth."

When Fun Meant Cheat

As they read, dictionary editors watch for other developments in the language besides the entry of new words. One of these developments is an oddity—how people in different parts of the country use different words to describe the same thing.

In Boston, for example, a dry-cleaning establishment is known as a "cleanser." In Minnesota, a rubber band is a "rubber binder." A sandwich of many ingredients in a small loaf of bread is known as a "poor boy" in New Orleans, a "submarine" in Boston, a "hoagy" in Philadelphia, a "hero" in New York City, and a "grinder" in upstate New York. In Milwaukee, people use a "bubbler"; most other Americans use a drinking fountain.

Another development editors watch for is how words change meaning—although this is a process that usually takes generations. Here are some examples:

Blizzard changed from a "sharp blow" in 1829 to, almost forty years later, the definition it has kept to this day: "A snowstorm with high winds."

In 1685, *fun* was a verb—"I funned him." It meant "to cheat, hoax, cajole, make a fool of." Today, *fun* is used as a noun—"We had fun in class."

Gossip started out in 1601 as a sponsor in a baptism "—to give a name to." Only twenty-six years later, in 1627, it was used in the sense of "to talk idly, mostly about other people's affairs."

Pretty went from "sly" to "clever" and only recently to "beautiful."

Cad started out as a passenger without a ticket on a coach. It changed to "an assistant, such as a bricklayer's helper," then to "a collector of fares on a bus," and only recently to "a fellow of low and vulgar manners."

Here are some other words that have changed meaning over many years and what they originally meant:

cunning—knowledge or skill

insolent—unusual

outlandish—foreign

pretend—assert rightly or wrongly

villain—a farmer

nice—ignorant

blackguard—a kitchen helper who guarded black pots and pans in a noble's kitchen, then a soldier dressed in black, next a bootblack, now a rascal

rascal—a plain, common soldier

idiot—a plain, common citizen

Recently, dictionary editors noted a meaning shift in *cheerfully*. For many years, people used it to mean "being in good spirits; happy." Then an editor noted the following use of the world in an advertisement: "Your money will be cheerfully refunded." He made out a citation slip, noting that *cheerfully* was used in the sense of "ungrudgingly." If *cheerfully* continues to be used in this sense, the usage will appear in a future dictionary.

In April 1971, the *Wall Street Journal* carried a story on a United States Ping-Pong team that had gone to China. The story included the phrase, "Ping-Pongers' visit to Peking . . ." If people begin to use *Ping-Ponger* to mean someone who plays Ping-Pong, this term, too, will someday appear in a dictionary.

Many words in our language take on more than one meaning or usage, and dictionary editors must be alert to each one of them. *Space,* in a desk dictionary, has nine different uses, from "The expanse in which the solar system, stars, and galaxies exist" to "Reserved accommodation on a public transportation vehicle" —as in "space (a seat) reserved on an airplane."

In some unabridgeds, *run* has 109 uses. The champion, though, is *set*—213 (although only 60 or so appear in most desk dictionaries).

New words enter the language, others change meaning, and still others—having outgrown their usefulness—simply drop out.

Your grandparents used *nickelodeon, Victrola, icebox,* and *buggy whip.* But nickelodeons have been replaced by motion pictures, Victrolas by the record player, iceboxes by refrigerators, and buggy whips—well, people drive cars today instead of a horse and wagon.

Does anything stay the same in our language? About the only thing that stays constant is change. Like a stream, English is the same from day to day even while it's changing. The job of dictionary makers is to watch the stream of language and carefully and painstakingly record the changes they see.

Ghoti Spells Fish

Probably the toughest job in making a new dictionary is to establish the pronunciation of words. To assist in the task, editors consult language specialists called phoneticians.

From listening to the radio and TV, phoneticians know that many words have different pronunciations depending usually on the part of the country in which the word is used. *Often,* for example, is usually pronounced with a silent *t—off-fen.* Recently, though, people have been sounding the *t—off-ten.* Some phoneticians say that this new form will gradually replace the silent *t* version.

Suite—as in bedroom suite—is another example. In some regions, it is pronounced *sweet* and *suit* in others. Which pronunciation will finally prevail only time will tell.

Both English pronunciation and spelling are difficult for students of English. With other languages—Spanish, Finnish, Bohemian, and to some extent German and Italian—it's possible to look at a word and know how it will sound. But not so with English. In our language, pronunciation doesn't correspond to spelling and gives no end of difficulty, not only to foreign-born people trying to learn English but to Americans trying to spell their own language as well.

Here are a few examples:

The English *sh* sound has 14 different spellings: *shoe, sugar, issue, mansion, mission, nation, suspicion, ocean, nausea, conscious, chaperon, schist, fuchsia,* and *pshaw.*

Silent letter combinations are another bugaboo. Back before Shakespeare's time, silent letters were pronounced. The *gh* in *thought,* for example, came out as a gargled *thocht.* The *ight* in *right* and *night* were also given the sound of *icht.* Although our pronunciation of these silent letter combinations has changed, our spelling hasn't followed suit.

Note, too, how the *oo* sound in the following words is the same but has five different spellings: *blue, crew, shoe, through, too.*

On the other hand—just to confuse things—English uses the same spelling for nine different sounds. Say *ough* in the following words: *tough, though, thought, thorough, bough, cough, drought, hiccough.*

Then come the homonyms—words that sound alike but are spelled differently: *pair—pear; beat—beet; meat—meet; grate—great; peace—piece; sew—so; there—their—they're.*

The 26 letters in our alphabet can produce 117 different English sounds. Even *a* has seven different sounds: *art, ape, fat, fare, fast, what, all.* And sometimes even *e* sounds like *a: obey.*

The ultimate absurdity of English spelling, however, was suggested by George Bernard Shaw, an English writer. He showed that the word *ghoti* could be pronounced "fish." Here's how:

Pronounce the *gh* like *f* in *cough* or *rough*. The *o* like the short *i* in *women*. The *ti* like *sh* in *nation*.

The result? Fish!

"It is unfortunate," said one dictionary maker, "that our orthography bears so little relation to our phonology."

The Longest Words

One curiosity of language that dictionary editors constantly watch for is long words, but not any long words. They watch for the longest words in the English language. Over the years they have come across some real jawbreakers.

For many years, the record was held by the 28-letter *antidisestablishmentarianism.*

This was replaced by a 29-letter word meaning "estimation as worthless"; *floccinaucinihilipilification.*

The 34-letter nonsense word used to represent the longest word in the language from a modern song and motion picture now fits in here: *supercalifragilisticexpialidocious.*

Then a reader came across a medical term for an obscure lung disease afflicting miners, the 45-letter *pneumonoultramicroscopicsilikovolcanikoniosis.*

But the longest English word ever to appear in print was a 51-letter jawbreaker used by an eighteenth century English physician to describe the water at a health resort at Bristol. He described it as *aqueosalinocalcalinocetaceoaluminosocupreovitriolic.*

Lost to literary history forever, though, was how he pronounced his awesome word.

It's unlikely that you'll ever find all of these words in any dictionary. Why? Because they are "nonce words," words used once or twice, perhaps written by only one person, and then not used again. But each one, at one time or another in the lively history of the English language, has appeared to baffle and amuse readers.

What Is "Good English"?

Does the dictionary tell us how to use "good English"? Many people think it does. But the answer may surprise you. Some dictionaries do and others do not.

There is a good reason why this is so. Today's dictionary makers are sharply divided about what a dictionary should do for its readers.

One group says this:

"The purpose of a dictionary is not to dictate—or even recommend—how people should use words. The term 'good English' is misleading. It suggests that someone, somewhere, dictates what is 'good' and 'bad' about the language we speak, read, and write. There is no such authority—nor is the dictionary that authority!

"A dictionary has one purpose only—to record the language. Let me quote that great English lexicographer, Dean Richard Trench, founder of *The Oxford English Dictionary*. In 1857, Dr. Trench gave what we believe to be the best statement yet on the function of the dictionary: 'A dictionary . . . is an inventory of the language. It is no task of the maker of it to select the good words of a language. If he fancies that it is so, and begins to pick and choose . . . he will at once go astray. . . . He is an historian [of the language], not a critic.'

"All words are good. Usage depends on what groups they're used in. In some groups, *ain't* is perfectly acceptable, but *sesquipedalian* or *photosynthesis* are not. In other groups, just the opposite would be true. Every group, every social situation, has its own standards for what is correct and incorrect. It's up to people to apply their intelligence and education to the truth on the dictionary page before them and decide whether a particular word fits a particular situation."

The second group of dictionary makers says this:

"There *is* such a thing as good English! It means grace and precision in the use of words. It keeps the language from back-sliding. We should all try to achieve it.

"The role of the dictionary is to offer readers guidance in the use of words, to say what is acceptable and what is unacceptable. While there may be no one person to say what is 'good English,' there are people who can guide us—writers, poets, editors, and teachers who work with words everyday and who enjoy using the tools of their trade correctly, like a good cabinetmaker insisting on a sharp wood chisel. They can give the dictionary user an informed opinion on what is acceptable or unacceptable. People go to the dictionary for that purpose.

"We don't nit-pick over language. We recognize that language changes. But it's our job to help the language grow by welcoming any new word that brings it strength or color. But we must keep the language from becoming sloppy. *Dropout* is a fine addition to our language. It's expressive and fills a real need. But *ain't* is unacceptable—no matter where it's used or what group uses it.

"People look for guidance in using the words of our language and it's up to the dictionary to give it to them."

The debate between the two groups is likely to go on without a truce or settlement. The public knows little about these fierce debates over words that go on daily among people whose job it is to study and record the language. But in the offices of dictionary publishers, in colleges and universities, in newspaper and magazine editorial offices, in radio and TV stations—wherever words are the tools of making a living—people will argue over words the way the rest of the population argues over religion and politics. Consider *contact,* for example.

The argument over the use of this seven-letter word has raged in word circles for almost half a century. Up to about 1930, people used *contact* solely as a noun. It meant "the coming together or touching of two objects or surfaces." ("The contact between the two electrodes . . .") Then people began using *contact* in a new way, as a verb, in the sense of "communication with another person or agency." ("I'll contact you as soon as I get in town . . .")

The uproar among writers, editors, and dictionary makers about using *contact* as a verb went unnoticed by the public who, if they did hear about it, might have dismissed the whole debate with, "What's the big fuss?" But word people felt differently. One magazine editor said, "If an applicant uses *contact* as a verb when applying for a job, forget him!"

The row even got into newspapers like *The New York Times* and the *Herald Tribune*. One story in 1931 told of an executive in a large company who wrote the following memo to his employees: "Somewhere there cumbers this fair earth with his loathsome presence a man who for the common good should have been destroyed in early childhood. He is the originator of the hideous vulgarism of using *contact* as a verb."

Despite the resistance of word experts, *contact* as a verb has worked its way into dictionaries. Seven out of ten word experts, though, still shudder at using the word as a verb. In dictionaries that guide readers in usage, they advise that *contact* as a verb is "not appropriate."

What does this debate—and the debate over all other words—come down to? Simply this. It points up the remarkable strength of English—a language that is flexible enough to absorb and support more than one viewpoint and free enough so people can use it confidently with all degrees of skill and learning. It's a language for a class in English literature and for the street, a language for mechanics and scholars, for movie makers and religious leaders, for lawyers and sportscasters, for judges and shopkeepers, for school children and school teachers. English is a remarkable instrument for playing everyone's song.

Chapter Eight

Dictionaries
for Boys and Girls

One of the grand events in dictionary-making history took place
in 1935. In that year, the *Thorndike-Century Junior Dictionary*
was published. Special about this dictionary was that it was the
first dictionary written exclusively for school children.

Edward L. Thorndike, the man who created this special dictionary, was a teacher at Teacher's College, Columbia University,
in New York. Interested in children and the way in which they
learned to read, he was concerned about the difficulty they had
using dictionaries.

Thorndike had good reason to be concerned. Dictionaries up
to the mid-1930s were written only for adults, but not even adults
could read them comfortably. They found definitions hard to
read and understand. People looking up "kangaroo," for example,
came upon this definition: "A herbivorous leaping marsupial
mammal of Australia and adjacent islands."

After puzzling over this definition, the looker-uppers would
locate "herbivorous" to find out what that meant, then "marsupial,"
and finally "adjacent." If by that time they weren't thoroughly con-
fused and wondering why they had bothered in the first place,
they turned back to "kangaroo" and gamely tried to figure out
just what kind of animal it was.

Thorndike changed all that. A kangaroo, he wrote, was "an
animal that lives in Australia. It has small forelegs and very
strong hind legs which give it great leaping power. The mother

kangaroo has a pouch in front in which she carries her young."

Although it may seem obvious today, Thorndike introduced the principle of clear definitions into dictionary making. No longer was "fable" a "fictitious narrative." Thorndike said, simply and clearly, that it was "a story that is not true." An agate—the kind used in a game of marbles—he changed from "a variegated chalcedony" to "a stone with colored stripes or clouded colors." Dictionaries he believed should be written clearly so that all readers, children or adults, would know what they were reading.

Another important contribution to dictonary making that Thorndike made was so commonsensical that we wonder today why no one ever thought of it earlier.

Older dictionaries—before 1935—always gave the size of animals as a fraction of the drawing of the animal that illustrated the definition. Thus, an inch-long drawing of a hippopotamus, for example, was described as "$\frac{1}{80}$" of the animal's true size.

Have you ever tried multiplying a one-inch picture of a hippopotamus eighty times to get an idea of its true size? Dictionary makers expected your parents and grandparents to have this extraordinary ability.

Thorndike changed that, too. Below the drawing, he stated that the size of a hippopotamus was "about 13 feet long." Generations of dictionary users have been grateful to him for that.

When he began planning his first dictionary for children, Thorndike came up against another problem: what words to include in the dictionary. Up to this time, most small- and medium-sized dictionaries were simply cut-down versions of the big unabridged dictionaries that carried up to 600,000 words. What words to include in smaller dictionaries—like desk or pocket dictionaries—was simply a matter of opinion.

Thorndike felt that a dictionary for school children should include words that they were most likely to come upon in their reading—"a dictionary to fit the learner," he said. But no one knew what these words were.

Therefore, Thorndike and a group of readers began reading—

books, textbooks, magazines, newpapers. They read 30 million words, and, as they read, they counted the words most often used in English.

They discovered that the first ten words in order of use are *the, and, a, to, of, I, in, was, that,* and *it.* The 70th word was *man.* *Woman* was the 207th word most frequently used.

From this word count, Thorndike published lists of the 10,000, 20,000, and finally the 30,000 words most frequently used in the English language.

Here, for the first time in five hundred years of dictionary making, was a way of building a dictionary from the bottom up— by including words that school children would most likely come across in their studies. From these lists, Thorndike built four school dictionaries: *Beginning, Junior, Revised Junior,* and *Senior.*

But no dictionary—and Thorndike realized this—could follow a strict system of including words that appeared on word lists only. For any group—primary graders or senior high students— this would limit language too rigidly. Therefore, Thorndike included enough uncommon words and meanings to perk the curiosity of youngsters using his books and to quicken their interest in words.

Today, as a result of Thorndike's work, dictionaries are available for youngsters of all ages. Some examples: Xerox Family Education Services' *The Weekly Reader Beginning Dictionary* (grades 2 and 3) and *The Xerox Intermediate Dictionary* (grades 4-8); Harcourt Brace Jovanovich's *Harcourt Brace Intermediate Dictionary* (10-16 years); Pyramid Publications' *Primary Dictionary Series—Dictionary 1* (4-6 years), *Dictionary 2* (6-8 years), *Dictionary 3* (8-10 years), *Dictionary 4* (10-12 years). This last is a set of four paperback dictionaries.

Five Million Words by Computer

In 1972, thirty-seven years after Edward Thorndike published his landmark dictionary, another important dictionary for children was published. *The American Heritage School Dictionary* —35,000 entry words, 1,024 pages, for grades three through nine— selected words with the help of a computer. It was also the first dictionary written to avoid sexism—favoritism toward one sex to the neglect of the other.

The editors at American Heritage had never produced a dictionary for school children before. They had, however, produced one of the most successful of all home/office dictionaries. Published in September 1969, *The American Heritage Dictionary of the English Language* immediately became a best-seller. It sold 440,000 copies before the end of the year and outsold every new book published that year. It ended up 1970 as the seventh best-selling book among all non-fiction titles published, a remarkable record for a dictionary.

When the editors began planning a dictionary for children, they didn't want to do a cut-down version of their big 155,000-word, 1550-page best-seller. Instead, they asked themselves two questions: "What words should a dictionary present for boys and girls in grades three through nine? What words do they see in their reading at home and in school that they would likely want to look up?"

The editors might have turned to Thorndike's original word lists, but they knew these lists were no longer up to date. The language had changed radically since Thorndike's time. Youngsters saw words in books, magazines, and newspapers that weren't in existence when Thorndike wrote his dictionary—*Afro, air piracy, area code, far-out, flashcube, low profile, maxi, midi, moonscape, Ms., pantsuit, recycle, rip-off, Wankel engine, way out, wind down, zero population growth.*

To find out exactly what words young people in grades three through nine were reading, the editors undertook a huge project. They read over a thousand textbooks, workbooks, novels, poetry books, encyclopedias, and magazines that boys and girls in these grades read. From this material, they randomly selected 10,000 blocks of 500 words each. This "corpus" of five million words served as the body of words youngsters came into contact with every day.

For the next six months, computer experts converted all five million words to two hundred reels of magnetic tape. Along with each word block, they added coded reference information—the book or magazine in which a passage appeared, page number, line number, and grade level.

Then, with all five million words coded into the computer, a computer operator gave the following instructions:

"First, arrange all words in alphabetical order. Next, rank them in order of frequency—that is, tell me what word is used most often, the next most often, and so on. Finally, print out a three-line citation slip for each word. Skip citation slips for function words—like *a, of, the, as.* I don't want them. But for all other words, I'd like a citation slip—a three-line statement in which each word is used. Also, tell me what grade the word is used in. Okay, get started."

The operator punched a button and the amazing machine went to work. The results—the printed output of the computer—filled seven volumes. Here are some of the computer's findings:

* The five million words thinned out to 87,000 individual word forms. Where we would call *walk, walked, walking,* and *walks* one word, the computer counted four different word forms.

* The most often used word was again *the.* It occurred about once in every 13 words—373,106 times—about twice as much as *of* and *and.*

* The ten most-often-used words were almost the same as Thorndike's top ten almost forty years earlier: *the, of, and, a, to, in, is, you, that, it.*

* In the first hundred most-often-used words, there were only four nouns: *time, people, water, words.*

* The most frequently used verbs were *is, was,* and *are.*

* The most frequently mentioned occupations were *scientist, teacher,* and *farmer.*

* *Money* occurred more often than *love, car* more than *family,* *war* more than *peace*, *Republican* more than *Democrat*, *up* more than *down*, *right* more than *wrong* or *left*.

* The days of the week most often used were *Saturday* and *Sunday*.

* *White* was the color most often mentioned followed by *red*, *black*, *green*, and *blue*.

* *May* was the most popular month, *December* the least popular.

* The two names most often used were *John* and *Mary*.

* Here are seven words and the frequency with which they occurred in the five million word corpus:

> take—4,089
> brain—382
> Chinese—341
> Russian—236
> yeah—79
> aw!—35
> huh!—23

* Thirty-four thousand words appeared only once: *dropouts*, *underachievers*, *hightail*, *trespasses*, and *goody-goody*.

* But *metamorphosis* occurred six times in third grade reading materials—usually in stories about caterpillars changing into butterflies.

Along with word-frequency counts, the computer typed out 700,000 three-line citations. Although fast, the computer was not smart. It responded to letters in certain sequences but not to the words themselves. It couldn't tell the difference between *lead* as in the "lead actor" in a play from *lead* in "lead pencil," a *row* of seats from a *row* between friends, and a *business deal* from a *good deal.*

But the computer's inability to distinguish between word meanings presented no problem for the dictionary editors. They found that the three-line citation slips for each word practically sorted

An editor looks over some of the hundreds of publications read each year by the editorial staff of a dictionary publisher to find new words, new uses of words in current use, and other changes in the language. (G. & C. Merriam Company)

Each new usage of a word spotted by an editor is noted on a 3 x 5 card, called a citation slip. It lists the word, the sentence in which it is used, the form of the word, the author's name, the publication in which it appeared, and the page and column number and date. Here is a citation slip for the word *Euclidean*. (G. & C. Merriam Company)

One bank of the file holding 12 million citation slips at the G. & C. Merriam Company. Some citations go back 70 or 80 years and reflect how a word changes over the years. (G. & C. Merriam Company)

To write a definition, an editor consults all the citation slips that have accumulated for a word. The slips show the variety of ways in which people use the word. Citation slips are used for the constant re-examination and revisions of definitions necessary to produce a new dictionary. (G. & C. Merriam Company)

A phonetician listens to recordings of speeches. By listening to radio and TV broadcasts, he picks up changes in the pronunciation of words. He prepares a pronunciation key for a dictionary and, after each word, gives a phonetic spelling to show readers how to sound out the word. (G. & C. Merriam Company)

These shelves hold books and magazines for third through ninth graders from which 10,000, 500-word samples were chosen. From this body of 5,000,000 words that students in these grades come upon in their reading, the editors—with the help of computers—selected 35,000 entry words to appear in *The American Heritage School Dictionary*. (Houghton Mifflin Company)

Two computer-typed citation slips for "major" and "majoring." These three-line citations, each beginning in the middle of a sentence, came directly from reading materials for third through ninth graders. (Houghton Mifflin Company)

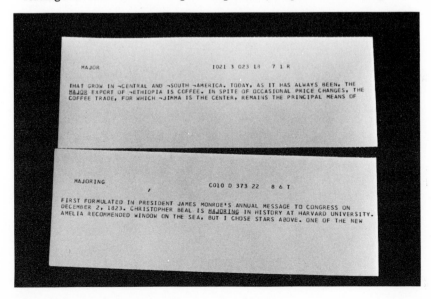

An editor lifts out citation slips for the word "box." (Houghton Mifflin Company)

A stylebook. Editors use this reference notebook to assure that the writing style in *The American Heritage School Dictionary* will be consistent throughout. A close-up of one page shows an instruction to editors for presenting inflected forms of entry words in boldface type. An inflected form is an alteration of a word—the *'s* in *girl's,* for example, to show possession, or *ran* as the past tense of *run.* (Houghton Mifflin Company)

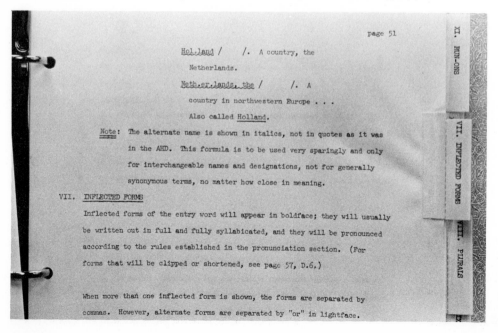

XI. RUN-ONS

Holland /   /. A country, the

Netherlands.

Netherlands, the /   /. A

country in northwestern Europe . . .

Also called Holland.

Note: The alternate name is shown in italics, not in quotes as it was

in the AHD. This formula is to be used very sparingly and only

for interchangeable names and designations, not for generally

synonymous terms, no matter how close in meaning.

VII. INFLECTED FORMS

Inflected forms of the entry word will appear in boldface; they will usually

be written out in full and fully syllabicated, and they will be pronounced

according to the rules established in the pronunciation section. (For

forms that will be clipped or shortened, see page 57, D.6.)

When more than one inflected form is shown, the forms are separated by

commas. However, alternate forms are separated by "or" in lightface.

VII. INFLECTED FORMS

VIII. PLURALS

Editors and art directors review photographs of bird beaks. They will select one photograph to illustrate the entry for *beak* in the dictionary. (Houghton Mifflin Company)

An editor examines a galley—a typeset section of the text for a book. A galley allows editors to find and correct errors in the text before the book is paged, plated, and printed. (Houghton Mifflin Company)

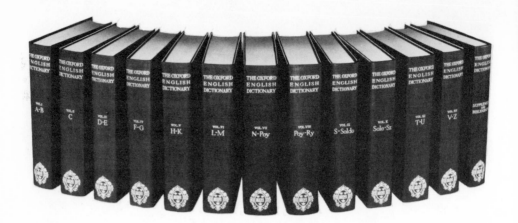

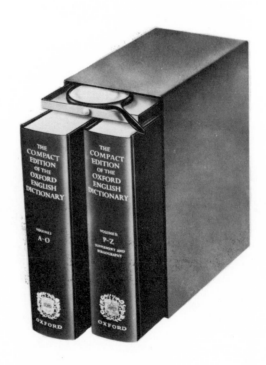

Some of the major dictionaries published today: *The Oxford English Dictionary,* the king of dictionaries, consists of 13 volumes that weigh 105 pounds and contains virtually all the words used in the English language since 350 years before Columbus discovered America. (Oxford University Press) By means of a photographic process that reduced the pages of the original edition, the two-volume *The Compact Edition of the Oxford English Dictionary* was made. A magnifying glass helps users read the text. (Oxford University Press) *The Random House Dictionary of the English Language* contains 260,000 words in 2,090 pages. (Random House) *Webster's Third New International Dictionary,* containing over 450,000 words, took ten years to complete. (G. & C. Merriam Company)

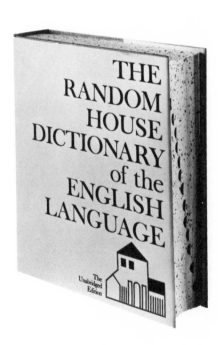

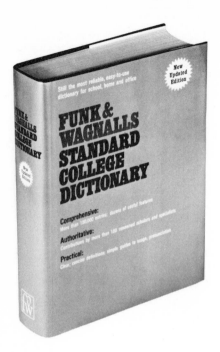

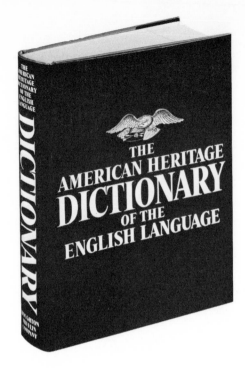

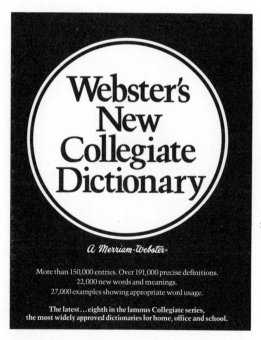

Three of the smaller dictionaries designed for use in home, office, or school: *Funk & Wagnalls Standard College Dictionary* contains more than 150,000 entries. (Funk & Wagnalls) *The American Heritage Dictionary of the English Language* presents 155,000 entry words in 1,550 pages. (Houghton Mifflin Company) *Webster's New Collegiate Dictionary,* the eighth in the famous Collegiate series, contains more than 150,000 entries. (G. & C. Merriam Company)

themselves into stacks for each use and part of speech. Out of 550 citations for *check*, for example, 479 were verbs ("Check these figures") and only 71 were nouns ("Please write a check for five dollars").

The task then of actually writing definitions was made much easier. The editors consulted additional word sources to write definitions, but they used sentence illustrations for each word directly from the citation slips and thus created a dictionary from materials that students would be familiar with.

Here is an example of a three-line citation printout for one use of the word *dean* and the accompanying code.

dean   U160   1   004   14   5   4   R

counsel in 1862. He served as counsel for the Canadian Pacific Railway from 1880 to 1887, when he became a director. For several years he was *dean* of the Faculty of Law at McGill University. He held the office of mayor of

The reference code at the top translated as follows:

U—library general reference
160—Compton's Picture Encyclopedia, Vol. 1
   (entry: Sir John Abbott)
1—1st sample
004—page 4
14—approximate line number
5—fifth grade
4—public, independent, and Catholic schools
R—general reference

Different code letters meant different things. An A at the beginning of the code line meant a general reading book. At the end, an F meant "fiction," T meant "textbook," and X meant "magazine."

When editors analyzed the word-frequency list, it revealed what lexicographers had long suspected—that the English language favored the male of the species.

The list revealed that *he* was number 11 while the word *she* ranked 54th. *Man* was 113 whereas *woman* was 719. Both *he* and *his* scored in the top twenty most-frequently-used words, but *her* was 64. *Boy* and *boys* were used 4,700 times to 2,200 times for *girl* and *girls*. *Man/men* outnumbered *woman/women* 7 to 1, this despite the fact that, in the real world, women outnumber men 100 to 95.

Sexism—discrimination toward members of one sex by another— is so ingrained in our language that we don't think about it. The leader of a committee is a chairman. If the leader is a woman, she's still a chairman. Our juries are twelve-man juries, even when women make up a majority of the members. We say, without really thinking, "A scientist is a man who has dedicated himself . . ." Many scientists today are women. And what if a woman fell overboard from an ocean liner? Without a moment's hesitation, most of us would yell, "Man overboard!"

Over the past few years, women have rebelled against this thoughtless favoritism to men shown by our language and in our society. Gradually English is changing to put the matter right. *The American Heritage School Dictionary* was the first school dictionary to reflect these changes.

To illustrate words like *drive* and *sole*, the editors wrote, "Her drive and ambition will help her get ahead" and, "She took sole command of the ship." In similar sentences in earlier editions of school dictionaries, *he* and *his* would have been used. For *show*, the editors wrote: "'I'll show them,' she muttered. 'I'll make a home run!'"

In the AHSD, girls instead of boys use a *microscope, rake,* and *shovel*. In illustrations, they *leapfrog*, do *handstands* and *cartwheels*, walk on *stilts*, and play the *English horn*.

The editors also steered away from the way we traditionally view boys and men. For *teach* and *well*, they wrote: "He teaches kindergarten" and, "Tears welled up in his eyes."

Youth is defined as "the time of life before one is an adult" not as "the time of life between childhood and manhood." A *sage* is not "a wise and venerable man," but "a very wise person, usually old and highly respected."

By dividing examples of words almost evenly between male and female and refusing to favor either sex, the editors show the reader another change in our ever-evolving language.

Chapter Nine

The English Language Today: "Language of Live Men"

When William the Conqueror crowned himself King of England in 1066, only 1.5 million people spoke English. And five hundred years later, in 1582, a famous teacher named Richard Mulcaster wrote, "The English tongue is of small reach, stretching no further than this island of ours."

Today, English is the most widely spoken language in the world. Three hundred million people speak it as their native tongue, and another 700 million claim it as a second language. Used on every continent, English is the language of statesmen, scientists, and scholars. Every religion and race uses it.

More people speak Chinese than English as their native tongue —nearly 500 million—but these people are largely confined to one country. English is followed by Hindustani, Spanish, Russian, and German in the number of people who use them either as first or second languages. In George Washington's day, French was the world's foremost language. In two hundred years' time, however, French has sunk to seventh place.

English is the language of pilots who fly international aviation routes. Pilots and control tower operators can communicate more efficiently—and clearly—in English. For air/ground talk, it's easier to say "jet" than *avion à réaction,* for example, and "flaps" than *volets de flexions.*

Seventy percent of the world's mail is addressed and written in English. More than 60 percent of the world's radio programs are broadcast in English.

Crates of goods made in Russia and sent to other countries are labeled "Made in U.S.S.R."—in English. Schools in Russia offer English courses from the fifth grade on.

Almost every capital city in Asia and Africa has an English-language newspaper.

In Teheran, over a hundred private language schools give lessons in English. Their slogan is: "If you don't know English, you know nothing."

In 1963, a professor in a Paris university complained—after noting that 5,000 American words and 30,000 technical terms had entered French—"If we do not take care now, in forty years' time, the French language will have ceased to exist!"

Ten years later, the French government declared that, henceforth, certain American expressions would no longer be allowed in government reports. French was the language of the country, and the government insisted that its employees use it. By official order, the government replaced "jumbo jet" with *grosporteur,* "spacecraft" with *astronef,* "bulldozer" with *bouteur* or *bouldozeur,* "flashback" with r*étrospectif,* and "one-man show" with *spectacle solo.*

What will happen if some clerk still insists on using the English word instead of its French replacement? A high government official looked grim as he replied to the question. "He will be put right by his superior," he said.

Why English Succeeded

In the world today, people speak 4,000 different languages, but only 5 percent—about 200—are recorded in written form.

Why, among all languages, did English succeed in becoming the world's first language? Why did a language that began with Germanic tribes settling on a green island across a twenty-one-mile channel of water from the mainland succeed in 2,500 years, whereas older languages—Chinese, German, Spanish, and French —stopped short of becoming world languages?

The first reason was the expansion, over two centuries, of the British Empire into almost all parts of the world, an expansion that reached its peak about World War I. During these decades, British government workers and soldiers introduced English into villages, towns, and cities in Europe, Africa, Asia, Australia, New Zealand, in islands in the Pacific Ocean and the Caribbean Sea, and in North, Central, and South America.

Further support for English as a world language came after World War II when American soldiers, sailors, and airmen were posted in many countries—in Japan and China, the Near East, Africa, and Europe. Thousands of children in those countries learned a basic English expression: "Hey, Joe, gimme gum!"

These servicemen brought their families from the United States to live with them—much like the Vikings who settled in England with their families ten centuries earlier. The Americans spoke English with shopkeepers, salesgirls, and policemen. So each day, people in these countries heard English spoken and saw it written.

Along with servicemen, U.S. government agencies set up offices in these countries. One agency, the United States Information Agency, established 239 centers in 106 countries. These centers distributed books and magazines—all written in English—to the people of these countries.

The second reason English became so popular was that people needed a common language to communicate. In India, for example, people speak fourteen different languages. English became a second language that people agreed to use in order to trade back and forth.

The same thing happened in Africa where hundreds of different languages—four hundred in West Africa alone—are spoken.

But the main reason that English became so widespread was the usefulness of the language itself. Since its beginnings in England twenty-five centuries earlier, it had become the most efficient instrument ever devised for people to communicate with each other.

Over a period of centuries, most languages grow in the direction of simplicity. During its existence, more than any other language, English has been revised, planed down, and polished. Today, English is less complicated than most primitive languages, like those spoken by Australian aborigines, Eskimos, or the stone-age tribes of New Guinea.

English is also more expressive than other languages. Through centuries of borrowing words from other languages, English has acquired a larger, more varied vocabulary. The storehouse of the English language holds a word or expression for almost any thought people are capable of thinking, any object they are capable of viewing, or any condition they are capable of getting themselves into. Poets use the language and so do scientists, shopkeepers, lawyers, religious leaders, and newspaper boys. Jokesters can also use the language—as in the following tongue twister, the most difficult in the language:

The sixth sick sheik's sixth sheep's sick.

All of which shows how flexible our language is and how we can find words in it to express anything we want.

850 Words

Despite its extensive vocabulary, the genius of the English language lies in another direction.

Back in 1920, two Cambridge University scholars, I. A. Richards and C. K. Ogden, discovered a curious quality about the language. They discovered that just about any thought could be expressed in a mere 850 basic English words. They wrote a book on their discovery called *The Meaning of Meaning*.

Although there are 4,000 to 10,000 verbs in the vocabulary of the average college graduate, Ogden and Richards discovered that only 18 of these verbs were needed to communicate in English: *be, come, do, get, give, go, have, keep, let, make, may, put, say, see, seem, send, take,* and *will.*

In everyday conversation, we use only about a thousand basic words. Basic words plus basic verbs enable people in other countries to learn English easily as a second language.

Another reason why English is so easy to learn is that, unlike other languages, there are few rules governing the use of words. Almost any thought can be expressed in a simple word order that follows a basic subject, verb, and direct object order: I love you.

This basic structure, plus a thousand basic words, allows people in other countries to learn English more quickly than other languages. No other modern language has developed such a simple understructure and, because of this, no other language today finds itself on the tongues of over a billion people.

Each day dictionary makers observe this marvel of communication grow and change. Diligently they record it and arrange it so the rest of us can use it to convey our thoughts.

"Wondrous the English language," said that original recorder of words, Samuel Johnson, "language of live men!"

Selected Bibliography

BOOKS

Barnett, Lincoln. *The Treasure of Our Tongue.* New York: Alfred A. Knopf, 1964.

Epstein, Samuel and Beryl. *The First Book of Words.* New York: Franklin Watts, 1954.

Ernst, Margaret S. *Words: English Roots and How They Grew.* Third edition. New York: Alfred A. Knopf, 1954.

Morris, William and Mary. *Dictionary of Word and Phrase Origins.* New York: Harper & Row, 1962.

Nurnberg, Maxwell. *Wonders in Words.* Englewood Cliffs, N.J.: Prentice-Hall, 1968.

Partridge, Eric. *The Gentle Art of Lexicography.* New York: The Macmillan Company, 1963.

Sledd, James, and Ebbitt, Wilma R. *Dictionaries and That Dictionary.* Glenview, Ill.: Scott, Foresman and Company, 1962.

PERIODICALS

For readers of this book who are interested in pursuing the subject of dictionaries further, the author recommends checking the *Reader's Guide to Periodical Literature.*

For *The Story of the Dictionary,* the author read virtually all articles listed in the *Reader's Guide* for the past twenty-five years under two categories: "English Language—General" and "English

Language—Dictionaries." He also read other articles that caught his interest and applied to the subject. Articles listed in *Reader's Guide* offer the best way to keep up-to-date on the subject of how dictionaries record the living language.

OTHER READING

Dictionary publishers generously supplied the author with news releases on their new dictionaries and with booklets and pamphlets on the subject of dictionaries and the English language. One pleasure in writing this book was coming into touch with people who were both expert in and dedicated to their work.

Another source of information the author used was addenda in dictionaries. This front matter offers readers fascinating information not only on the history of language and who contributed to a dictionary, but also on another subject just as important—the editors' viewpoint in presenting the language. A reader discovers that dictionaries are no more alike than are dialects of English. The wonder of the language is that it absorbs all viewpoints.

Index

American Dictionary of the English Language, An, 17-18
American Heritage Dictionary of the English Language, The, 52. See also illustration
American Heritage School Dictionary, The, 52-57. See also illustrations
American Spelling Book, The, 15
Angles. See Anglo-Saxons
Anglo-Saxons, 28, 29

Bailey, Nathaniel, 9-10
Blue-Back Speller, 15-16

Caesar, Julius, 27
Cawdrey, Robert, 9, 10
Celts, 27, 28
Chesterfield, Lord Philip, 10, 11, 14
Churchill, Sir Winston, 27
Citation slips, 37-39, 40, 53-55. See also illustrations
Cockeram, Henry, 9, 10
Compact Edition of The Oxford English Dictionary, The, 24. See also illustration
Compendious Dictionary of the English Language, A, 16-17. See also illustration
Computers in dictionary making, 53-55
Cook, Captain James, 30

Dictionaries
for adults, 6-7, 36, 40
for children, 6, 49-57
history of, 8-25
kinds of, 5
number of words in, 6
popularity of, 5, 36
special features of, 35-36
unabridged, 6, 35-36
Dictionary making
citation slips, preparation and use of, 37-39, 40, 53-55. See also illustrations
computers used in, 53-55
costs, 35
inclusion of new words, 38-40
length of time required, 35, 36
principles governing children's dictionaries, 49-51, 52-53
pronunciation of words, 43-45
qualifications of editors, 41
and sexism, 55-57
writing word definitions, 40, 41-43
Dictionary of Difficult Words, A, 5
Dictionary of Embroidery Stitches, 5
Dictionary of Sea Slang of the Twentieth Century, 5
Dictionary of the English Language, A, 13-14. See also illustrations
Dictionary of the Underworld, 5
Drake, Sir Francis, 30

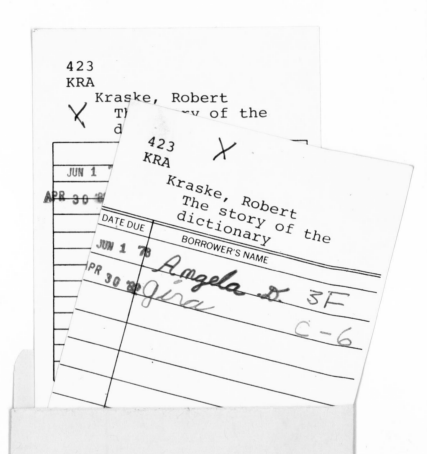

423
KRA

Kraske, Robert
The story of the
dictionary

DATE DUE	BORROWER'S NAME
JUN 1 7?	Angela D. 3F
APR 30 8?	gina
	C-6